HOW TO NETWORK WiTHOUT FEELING LiKE AN A-HOLE

HOW TO NETWORK WITHOUT FEELING LIKE AN A-HOLE

ANGELA GUIDO

Communicate Yourself Press

This book is for Vanessa,
the friendliest person I know

CONTENTS

INTRODUCTION

HI, I'M ANGELA!

HELLO THERE!!

———

Gosh, doesn't networking just make you feel like an a-hole sometimes? I mean, you know you need to meet people, you know connections help your career, you know it's who you know that counts. But when it comes right down to it, doesn't networking just kinda suck? You'd rather do just about anything than go to a networking event. And then when you get there, it's so easy to get bored or feel awkward. Then even if you do get that important business card of someone who can help, it just feels manipulative to reach out and ask for a favor!

I feel your pain. As an MBA, management consultant, and entrepreneur, I've always believed that networking is critically important. And that's coming from an introvert prone to occasional social awkwardness who despises small talk! I wasn't born a social butterfly—I taught myself how to become one, and now I'm going to show you how too. Believe me, I've always HATED networking. But as a student of human nature and coach to elite MBAs for the past 15 years, I've discovered something very interesting: pretty much everyone hates networking. You are not alone, my friend!

That's why I wrote this book. How to Network Without Feeling Like an A-Hole is designed to transform networking from a gross series of transactions into a fun and fulfilling way to build genuine professional friendships. Thousands of MBAs and aspiring business leaders around the world have created deeper self-confidence, greater social charisma, and more meaningful professional relationships using the tips and techniques I've shared in these pages.

Take, for example, what this one Harvard MBA student said:

"You know those people who rock networking events? The ones who are confident but not cocky, can float seamlessly from group to group, and somehow seem to be actual friends with the people you're there to network with? Angela made me one of those people. I'll never forget when a consultant at a top firm said to me at a large recruiting event, 'you're my rock at these things.' Thanks to the networking skills she taught me, I was granted interviews at all of my top-choice firms."

I promise if you follow this how-to guide, you'll become a super-connector with a thriving network of awesome professional friends. Networking will stop sucking and become an activity that enriches your life in unimagined ways. And you'll never have to look far for any career opportunity, because your network will be right there to support and champion you every step of the way.

True friendship blossoms over time, so if you want a great network, today is the day to start. A month from now, you'll hardly recognize yourself.

MAKE ME YOUR FIRST NETWORKING FRIEND!

If this book provokes any questions, please drop me a line. I'm always happy to hear from you. You can reach me and my team via this magical invention called email: questions@careerprotocol.com. Or on Instagram: @careerprotocol. And if I can be of service to you in any way on your quest for a career that inspires you, please just ask.

Finally, this book is about communication and forging real friendships with people in your professional life. That takes time. Time and email. I've put together a treasure trove of email templates you can use to deepen your own professional friendships. You can download them here: careerprotocol.com/emails.

Once you've grabbed those email templates, read on. Amazing professional friendships await!

WHY DO WE HATE NETWORKING?

01

NETWORKING IS IMPORTANT

It is something you HAVE to do. A strong network of friends and supporters is essential to a healthy career and a happy life. You've probably heard that the further you advance in your career, the more your relationships determine your opportunity set and ability to succeed. Check out this graphic.

The Sources of Your Professional Opportunities

Though your resume and experiences got you in the door through the first steps of your career (college, your first job, graduate school) the truism "It's not *what* you know; it's *who* you know" becomes more and more true as you advance to senior levels.

RESEARCH REPEATEDLY SHOWS THAT THE SINGLE BEST PREDICTOR OF WHETHER A CANDIDATE WILL GET THE JOB IS WHETHER HE OR SHE ALREADY KNOWS SOMEONE WHO WORKS AT THE TARGET COMPANY

If you think about it, this is just common sense. You will spend a third or more of your waking life at work. The people you work with will have a significant effect on your overall job satisfaction.

It's a simple fact that people want to work with people they like and people they trust. It's easier to like and trust someone who has a voucher from a friend or colleague.

What's more, the world's most interesting and important jobs are rarely publicized. Pretty soon, all the jobs you'll really want will be available by referral only.

SO YOU KNOW YOU HAVE TO NETWORK. BUT WHY DO MOST OF US CRINGE WHEN WE HEAR THE WORD?

The answer lies in the OTHER reason networking is important. Your relationships are not just a source of opportunities in your career, they're also the source of connection and an important driver of meaning and joy in your day-to-day life. Think about how much of your day you spend with other people. Think about how important your inner circle of friends and colleagues is to you. Think about all the happiness and fun you bring to each other's lives.

Consider the flipside: no matter how interesting and fun your work is, if you hate your boss, you're going to be miserable.

RELATIONSHIPS MATTER

And as human beings, we all want genuine relationships built on mutual trust, affinity, shared positive experiences, and generosity.

The problem with the conventional conception of networking is that it's transactional. You're supposed to go to the event, find the important people, sell yourself with an elevator pitch, collect cards, and then use those contacts to get ahead. Even the wisdom that tells us "You have to add value to your new contacts first before you can ask for something" is just an interim step in the manipulation—the idea being that if you give something first, you're entitled to get the thing you need. But it's still a paradigm based upon using people to get what you want. It's transactional.

FOR MOST OF US HUMANS, THIS MODEL OF NETWORKING WILL ALWAYS FEEL A BIT ICKY

Why? Because this perspective inherently forces us to value the transaction over the person, the individual gain over the connection, our own short-term needs over the possibility of genuine friendship.

There are two problems with this.

1. It's backwards. Generosity stems from genuine affinity and friendship. The people who know and like and trust us will naturally go out of their way to create opportunities for us. And these opportunities will be more meaningful because they'll be based on a history of understanding and shared values.

2. It feels bad. Networking with the intent to impress and subsequently take advantage of people just doesn't feel right. At best you'd likely feel smarmy and manipulative, but far more likely you'd feel fearful—of being judged, of being disliked, of being seen as a fraud. Trust your instincts. If you cringe when you think about "networking," you probably shouldn't do it. Feelings contain very important and valuable information about our values. Do not ignore your feelings.

> If you're approaching networking as something you have to do to forward your career and get what you want, you're inherently using people. That's the bottom line. The current networking paradigm is about utility, not connection.

BUT AS HUMAN BEINGS, WE DON'T ACTUALLY WANT TO USE PEOPLE

———

We'd rather be connected, share, and collaborate. We'd rather have real professional friendships. And professional friendships start with . . .

CONNECTION

———

Renowned researcher, storyteller, and TED Talker Brené Brown defines connection as follows:

CONNECTION is the energy that exists between people when they feel seen, heard, and valued; when they can give and receive without judgement; and when they derive sustenance and strength from the relationship.

This is a great way to think about connection. It's intangible; it's emotional; and you know it when it happens. And that's what this book is about. Creating and keeping connections!!

It's a new approach to networking that will allow you to begin building real professional friendships through networking events and all your other social activities.

IF YOU TRY THIS APPROACH, I
GUARANTEE YOU FOUR THINGS:

————

1. It will feel a lot better. You'll stop hating networking so much and look forward to events as a chance to meet new and interesting people who will one day become true friends.

2. You will get better at it. Instead of adding to a useless pile of business cards, you will begin cultivating real friendships that add meaning and joy to your life (and help advance your career).

3. You will have more confidence in yourself when speaking to strangers about who you are, what you value, and what you want.

4. Perhaps most importantly of all, you will have more fun!!!

5. So read on!! Your keys to building real professional friendships are already inside you. This book will help you bring them out, shine them up, and use them to your greatest advantage!

————

The only way to have a friend is to be one.

RALPH WALDO EMERSON

————

THE ANATOMY OF A FRIENDSHIP

02

THE ANATOMY OF A FRIENDSHIP

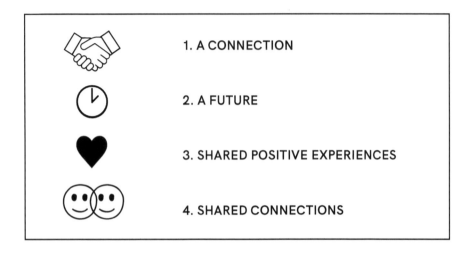

1. A CONNECTION

2. A FUTURE

3. SHARED POSITIVE EXPERIENCES

4. SHARED CONNECTIONS

THESE ARE THE FOUR COMPONENTS OF A REAL FRIENDSHIP

But this you already know, right? Look at every single relationship you have—family, friends, intimates, and professional connections. This is what they're made up of.

It starts with a chance meeting. In Hollywood, they call it a meet cute. It's the moment your eyes meet, and there you two are, face to face for the first time. It could happen anywhere, but in modern adult professional life, it happens most predictably at networking events. (That's what networking events are for!!! New meet cutes!) Not everyone you meet becomes a friend, though. To begin a relationship, you need a connection. Connection happens in a variety of ways, and this will be the focus of the next three chapters.

But not all the people you connect with become friends. That's because for the relationship to develop past that first chance meeting, it needs to have a future. And the best way to make sure it has a future is to create a context and a plan for the next interaction during the first one. We'll talk about this in Chapter 9.

Long-term relationships are based on shared positive experiences. The more experiences you share and the more positive they are as a whole, the deeper and more meaningful the relationship will be. Positive experiences happen all the time, and they're easy to create. In the modern era of email, LinkedIn, and Facebook, it's a little harder to understand exactly how to create positive SHARED experiences. These are the subject of Chapters 10 through 15.

The final component of all great friendships is shared connections. This is part of the reason you will rarely make better friends in life than you had in college and high school. Because those friendships developed within a shared network of connections—everyone was friends with everyone else, so relationships evolved quickly and to deeper levels. In adult life, we forget the importance of connecting others to others.

To make this really concrete for you, let's do a quick exercise.

2.1 LIST YOUR PROFESSIONAL FRIENDS

Make a list of at least 20 professional friends—that is, people you consider friends but whom you interact with primarily in a professional context. Include supervisors, managers, mentors, champions, peers, colleagues, people who work down the hall, fellow alumni, collaborators, clients, office managers, executive assistants, and anyone you have a relationship with that's meaningful.

Now take a moment and think about these questions for each person:

- How did you meet?

- What was your next step after that first meeting?

- What is at least one shared positive experience you have had?

- What is at least one shared connection you have (that is—someone you both know in common)?

2.2 FRIENDSHIP INSIGHTS

Take a moment and record your insights. What did you notice as you did this exercise? Are there some commonalities among your answers? Which friends do you consider the most important/closest/best? What did you notice about your answers to the questions about shared experiences and shared connections for those closest to you? Just reflect on any new ideas this exercise triggered.

2.3 WHAT DO YOU WANT?

Before you embark on this small journey to enhance your personal and professional relationships, take a moment and think about what you want to get from the rest of this book. Here are some ideas:

- I'd like to build 10 new important professional friendships this year.

- I want to be totally confident in my ability to network and make new connections!!

- I want to love networking!!

- I want to become recognized as a master connector and valuable asset to my whole network.

- I'd like to add 20 important people to my network in the next 3 months.

- I want to transition to a work environment where I am surrounded by people I really like.

- I want my upcoming job search to be fun!!

- But these are just some small ideas. Create your own and don't be afraid dream big!!

As we proceed through the chapters, I'm going to look at each of the problems people have with the conventional notion of networking and the typical challenges networking poses. I will reframe each experience in light of the anatomy of a real friendship and help you take a different approach to networking that is much more human and much more natural for you.

By the end of this short book, you'll have a new paradigm for networking and several new tools to begin building awesome professional friendships with everyone you meet that will enrich your life and your career. Pretty soon, you're going to be eager to attend those networking events that felt like so much drudgery before.

DOES NETWORKING TO GET A JOB MAKE YOU FEEL DESPERATE AND INSECURE?

03

So there you are—milling around in a huge group, appetizers in hand—trying to find the important people, and trying to make a good impression on the people who can help advance your career, while many other people are trying to do the same. At this point, you're probably thinking . . .

- How do I get the attention of the important people?

- How do I make a memorable impression when there are so many other people talking?

And if you've ever heard the advice that you "need to have your Elevator Pitch down and be able to sell your value proposition in 30 seconds or less," you're probably also thinking . . .

- What makes me so special professionally, and how can I convey it in a few seconds?

- How can I sell myself to this important person and that other important person?

- How can I impress everyone and look good?

And if you have even a modicum of self-awareness, you're probably also thinking . . .

- How can I do all that without looking, seeming, or feeling like a total douche, an arrogant ass, or an otherwise insensitive and socially awkward oaf?

The answer to this last question is your key: you can't.

When did networking events become an Egyptian Bazaar, people? When did we decide that when meeting people in a professional context, all common sense and genuine human ability to build relationships goes out the window in favor of hawking our wares and trying to manipulate others into liking us so we can use them for our purposes?

NO ONE WANTS TO USE OTHER PEOPLE

Just think about this logically. Consider some examples:

- If someone in class you've never seen before turns to you and asks for a copy of your notes, wouldn't you at least hesitate to say yes?

- If someone you just met asked you to counsel her on serious dating issues she was having, wouldn't you feel imposed upon?

- If on a first date, someone asked you to help him or her move into a new apartment, wouldn't you kick 'em to the curb?

- If you met someone at a benefit and that night she asked you on the spot for a $5,000 loan for her new entrepreneurial venture, wouldn't you seriously question her social savvy and soft skills?

Think about the nature of favors and how you feel when someone overreaches—asking for something that requires more trust and friendship than you already have. It's extremely off-putting.

And when someone is getting to know you just so that they can later ask you a favor, don't you know it?

We can all relate to the feeling of being used, and let's be honest—it sucks.

Since you're human, I know you don't actually want to use people. I know you'd rather connect, share, and collaborate. You'd rather people bring opportunities to you instead of chasing them. And you value your friends not because of what they can do for you but because of who they are.

So you need to honor the values of friendship and connection first when meeting new people at networking events.

PUT YOUR AGENDA ASIDE

Your common sense tells you that you can count on your friends and that you can't ask too much of strangers. So put your agenda aside with strangers until they become friends. This means that even if you have a genuine personal agenda (such as, "I need a job in the next two months!!"), you have to set it aside when you're meeting new people and just focus on making a genuine connection. If someone is going to be useful to your career, the time to discuss that is in a second, third, or fourth interaction.

"When meeting people for the first time, focus on connecting instead of selling."

Even if the networking event is a company sponsored meet-and-greet, the time to showcase your skills and achievements is in a subsequent interview when someone asks you questions like "Tell me about an accomplishment," or "Define your leadership style."

No, the time to tout accomplishments is not at a networking event. If you're in a room full of many other people who are mostly meeting for the first time, your objective is to connect, not to sell. So you have to temporarily suspend your personal agenda.

3.1 Agenda Exercise

So you can really get your agenda out of the way when you meet new people, try this exercise before a networking event.

What do you need right now in your career? (e.g. more mentors, a JOB!!!, an introduction to a recruiter at a company you want to work for, recommendations for training courses in coding, etc.). Make a list.

Then, put all of that aside. Park the list somewhere on your desk and forget about it. It will still be there when you get home AFTER you have made a few new friends.

3.2. Set a Friendship Intention

Now, after setting your agenda aside, create a new intention for this networking event/ opportunity/ day/ evening. Try stuff like:

—I intend to make two new friends tonight.

—I am going to focus on really getting to know at least five new people at this event.

—My goal is to be my authentic self and have fun sharing my experiences.

—(By the way, this is a cool exercise to do any and every day on all subjects! Write down what you want, set it aside, then set an intention to just do and feel good.)

When you are meeting new people, putting your attention on the person, sharing and listening, and building relatedness and affinity is common sense and human nature. It's what you would do if left to your natural devices. But unfortunately, some of the conventions of networking have disarmed us of our common sense and led us down a woeful path.

For example, the Elevator Pitch. Shudder.

DO ELEVATOR PITCHES MAKE YOUR SKIN CRAWL?

04

ELEVATOR PITCHES ARE UNCOMFORTABLE FOR EVERYONE, INCLUDING THE PEOPLE YOU'RE TRYING TO IMPRESS

———

Let me start with the history of this concept called the Elevator Pitch.

It started in . . . you guessed it . . . an elevator. The term has its origins in Hollywood. Screenwriters would hope to ambush studio executives in an elevator and pitch their script ideas in the 30-second ride to the penthouse suite.

Then business came in and coopted the term. Anyone in Silicon Valley, the Venture Capital Industry, or the entrepreneur community will tell you how important it is to be able to Elevator Pitch your business idea.

Today, professionals worldwide use an Elevator Pitch to quickly establish the value of an idea so they can get to the Ask. If there's no Ask, it's not an Elevator Pitch. In the case of a Hollywood executive, the Ask is a meeting or the chance to submit your full script for review. In the case of a Venture Capitalist, it's the opportunity to make a more thorough pitch of your business.

IT'S REALLY IMPORTANT TO UNDERSTAND TWO FEATURES OF A TRUE ELEVATOR PITCH

———

First, it's meant to interrupt someone and grab their attention. The studio exec wasn't planning to hear a pitch—she was just trying to get to her hotel room. The screenwriter has to be SO compelling so quickly because he is essentially being bullish and rude. He's interjecting his own agenda into someone else's life who was otherwise minding her own business.

Second, the point of an Elevator Pitch isn't really the idea itself; it's the Ask—the follow up opportunity. No one ever invested in a business or bought a screenplay in an elevator. The best they did was agree to consider buying it later.

The Elevator Pitch only exists to compel the listener to say "yes" to your Ask (and to do so while you are basically impolitely intruding on their space without permission.)

Here's how Investopedia defines the term: Elevator pitch is a slang term used to describe a brief speech that outlines an idea for a product, service or project. The name comes from the notion that the speech should be delivered in the short time period of an elevator ride, usually 20-60 seconds.

Read that again.

. . . a brief speech that outlines an idea for a product, service or project.

If you are an entrepreneur or ever find yourself in a role where you need to sell something—be it a process, a product, a service, an organization, or an event, please learn how to Elevator Pitch that thing.

But if the thing you are introducing is yourself, stop it.

You're not an idea, a product, a service, or a project. You're a complete human being, and an Elevator Pitch at best is selling you short.

ELEVATOR PITCHING YOURSELF DOESN'T WORK TO CREATE A CONNECTION.

———

Hopefully the discussion above foreshadowed the reasons you can't use an Elevator Pitch to introduce yourself at a networking event. But if it isn't crystal clear, just take a moment and reflect on your own experience trying to Elevator Pitch yourself (or your experience hearing someone else do so).

If you are like most people, when you tried to trot out a concise, memorized speech about how awesome you are to a group of strangers, at best you felt slightly awkward, but more likely, you felt like a total douche.

The reason for that is because . . .

An Elevator Pitch is designed to effect a transaction,
not to create a connection.

We are in the very important first stage of a real friendship: connection. And a connection won't transpire if the focus of the interaction is a transaction.

Just think about your interactions at a tollbooth. You pull up, hand over the change, and drive on. Even if you say "Hi, how are you?" have you ever really made a connection with a tollbooth operator? Did any one of them ever become a real friend? The answer is probably "No."

(By the way, this is one of the reasons tollbooth operators were once believed to have among the highest rates of suicide of any job. All day they have human interaction with no connection.)

We need and want to be connected. This is why the transaction approach to networking feels so bad on both the giving and receiving end.

THE ONE SITUATION WHERE AN ELEVATOR PITCH IS ALLOWED

Let's consider a single solitary situation in which an Elevator Pitch is the only alternative, and this will hopefully make it clear once and for all, why this is usually the wrong way to approach a personal introduction.

Imagine you just heard a stirring keynote address, and the speaker is on the way out to her car, but you'd really like to follow up for a specific reason. Let's say she leads a program at her company similar to one you lead and you want to discuss it with her. She's rushing out the door, so your only choice is to interrupt her and make a quick Ask.

Then and only then would an Elevator Pitch like this be appropriate:

"Hi Mary, my name is Angela, and I lead a training program for aspiring leaders through my company, Career Protocol. I was really inspired by the way you described the program you're leading at Executive Inc., and I'd love to talk shop about it. Could I have your card so I can email you to find a time to connect?"

THIS IS A TRUE ELEVATOR PITCH.

———

Notice how 60% of the words (the italics) are dedicated to the Ask and not to anything specific about me. Notice also that I'm not really making a connection here. In fact, I'm skipping the connection altogether and jumping to step 2 (creating a future—more on that in Chapter 9). I'll have to be mindful about creating a real connection later when I reach out to her, because it's unlikely she will be very enthusiastic to get my email (if she even remembers me).

THE CONNECTION STEP CANNOT BE SKIPPED IF YOU HOPE TO HAVE A REAL RELATIONSHIP.

———

Since Mary is in a hurry, and my only chance to speak with her in the future is to grab her card now, this Elevator Pitch is really my only choice. But under every other circumstance at a networking event, this kind of Elevator Pitch is a really bad idea for four reasons.

First, everyone is there to meet and interact. You shouldn't HAVE to interrupt people because all they are doing is standing around, talking and listening to each other. If you find yourself interrupting group conversations at a networking event to make your pitch to the important person, you've made a huge mistake. You may walk away with a business card, but you will have also left a stinky impression that you're someone who doesn't respect others and lacks emotional intelligence.

Second, remember, a networking event is not an Egyptian Bazaar. You aren't trying to sell yourself or your services. You already left your agenda at home, so the time to ask for favors, referrals, job interviews, etc. is later, in your second meeting or beyond. If you put your agenda out front, you are back to the "using people" paradigm that feels so bad.

Third, a big part of what we hate about networking in the first place is how bad it feels to be judged. When you're trying to sell yourself, convince others of your value, or make them like you, all you're really doing is opening yourself up for judgment. You're saying: "Here I am! Please find me good enough!" This is no way to start a relationship: it doesn't endear you to people nor does it bolster your own confidence or sense of self-affinity.

And finally, remember that your primary goal is to make a connection. Part of the reason the Elevator Pitch crept into networking conventions is because you do want to have a follow-up opportunity to speak with the people you meet (that's the Ask). But the notion that you have to convince them to do that by proving your value or by making sure they know "what's in it for them" makes it a transaction.

Helping people we like is its own reward for us human beings. Think about how good it feels to do something nice for a friend. Connection naturally leads to generosity. If people like you, they will want to talk to you again. If you make a connection, they will be amenable to follow-up. Your number one networking strategy is to make genuine connections.

AFRAID YOU WON'T MAKE A GOOD FIRST IMPRESSION?

05

Networking events are about making new meaningful human connections, building relationships, and getting to know people in a dynamic conversational environment. That means that true Elevator Pitching will fail almost every time.

In fact, the majority of your networking conversations won't focus on work, you as a person, or even any aspect of your professional life. Small talk is more likely to be the de rigueur discussion, so be sure to master that in Chapters 6 and 7.

Here is a good rule of thumb to follow:

Don't try to stand out in a group   **This is your moment to shine**

It's REALLY important to master small talk so that you can engage in a group conversation, go with the flow, listen and contribute, but not feel the need to hijack the discussion to focus on yourself. That will leave the opposite impression you want to leave, so be sure to read the next two chapters that deal with navigating group conversation gracefully.

But most people are at least a little bit nervous about this moment:

So let's talk about the moment someone turns to you and says "Tell me about yourself," or "What do you do?" Or that moment when, without a word, the group looks at you, and you know it's your turn to introduce yourself.

(Please, don't introduce yourself until you have the floor. If you don't know what I mean, be sure to read Chapter 7.)

The key to introducing yourself to anyone anywhere and engendering a real connection lies in this one concept:

Enthusiasm. Noun | en·thu·si·asm

"Strong excitement about something: a strong feeling of active interest in something that you like or enjoy."

Derived from the Greek enthousiazein, meaning "to be inspired."

—MERRIAM WEBSTER'S DICTIONARY

Think about it. This is your meet cute!! This conversation is the first step in what might be a lifelong friendship. This person could go on to become a very dear friend, a boss, a colleague, a collaborator, a travel buddy, a brother-in-law—who knows?

Whatever future your relationship holds, it will stand the greatest chance of being meaningful if you start it off right. This is your chance to make yourself known and to connect based on your own true values and what interests, excites, and inspires you. It's your chance to let others have a real glimpse into who you are.

WHAT DOES THIS MEAN FOR YOU?

Well, first of all, you probably shouldn't take this moment to recite a canned speech of any kind. We already ruled out the Elevator Pitch, but memorized speeches usually fall flat because they lack the vitality of spontaneity and presence.

And second of all, rather than emphasizing how awesome you are, stressing skills and accomplishments, touting bragging rights (all of which will likely make you seem and feel arrogant), you will be much better off if you connect on the basis of positive emotion instead of cold, hard facts. In the end, we humans are emotional beings, and our feelings have a lot more control over our preferences than our minds do.

We like people who make us feel good, not those we think we SHOULD like because they're so _____ (fill in the blank here with whatever positive qualities you think you have—smart/ capable/ accomplished/ whatever.)

Instead of trying to look good, letting your natural enthusiasm come through will positively affect everyone else around you because enthusiasm is contagious. As a result, others will inherently want to know you better.

SO INTRODUCE YOURSELF USING SOMETHING YOU'RE ENTHUSIASTIC ABOUT!

Choose something you love, something that makes your eyes light up, something that makes you come alive when you think and talk about it.

I do a lot of work with my clients to help them explore and understand their most deeply-held passions and values. This allows them to lead and communicate from a powerful place that is uniquely theirs and that results only from deep self-awareness.

So let's try a few exercises here to get you thinking about the things that you value, the things that make you come alive.

Here is our simple framework for personal and professional introductions to strangers:

	Past	Present	Future
Something you love	⟫⟫ →	● ●	● →
Something you want	⟫⟫ →	● ●	● →
Something you're curious about	⟫⟫ →	● ●	● →
Something that matters	⟫⟫ →	● ●	● →

LET'S CALL THIS YOUR ENTHUSIASM INTRODUCTION.

Here's how it works.

Step 1

Choose something you love, something you want, something you're curious about, or something that matters to you.

Let's make some lists.

5.1 Your Enthusiasms

Take 10 minutes right now and write out a list of:

1. Things you love.

2. Things that matter to you.

3. Thinks you are curious about.

4. Things you want.

Don't censor yourself, just write everything that comes to mind. Include the significant and the trivial, the recent and the lifelong, the professional and the personal.

Here is a partial list of my enthusiasms, for example:

THINGS I LOVE	THINGS THAT MATTER TO ME	THINGS I AM CURIOUS ABOUT	THINGS I WANT
Family			To enjoy the small things in life
Cheese	Humor	Neuroscience	
Storytelling	The fiber of global unity and interconnectedness	Italian cooking	To be a more loving person in every interaction
Travel		Physics (esp. quantum)	
Explaining complicated concepts in a simple way	Personal freedom for all	Astronomy	To grow my business
	Honest communication	Astrology	To help people fulfill their potential
Learning	Helping people communicate better	Languages	
		Human Nature	

Now, as you talk about yourself at a Networking Event, you can choose from anything on your lists. Customize the item you choose based on the context and who you're talking to.

Is it a corporate networking event for a company you're interested in working for? Talk about an aspect of your work that you love or your next professional desire (goal).

Are you at a benefit for supporters of your local animal shelter? Consider choosing a non-professional passion like the local restaurant scene or a certain kind of music.

If you're concerned about which topics might be taboo, be sure to read Chapter 8.

Step 2

Elaborate on that topic using the simple framework of time (past, present, and future).

Here is how that might sound. Let's take a quick example you might use at a social event. You just joined a group and they're engaged in small talk about travel. After a moment, everyone turns to you so you can make yourself known.

Thing you love: Travel

Past: I really love to travel too! I set a goal to visit 20 countries by the year 2020, and I have now been to 14!

Present: These days I'm really focused on work and haven't had the chance to get away in months.

Future: For my next trip, I'm eyeing Southeast Asia. Does anyone have destinations to recommend?

You can see how easily this lets you into a conversation that's already happening, talk about something meaningful to you, and then open the dialogue up to others. You will be remembered as an interesting person with genuine passions who invites the input of others.

If the conversation already in motion is focused on travel, hobbies, or leisure time, an introduction like this would be a perfect way to connect with the group and let the conversation go from there.

Importantly, though, this isn't meant to be a planned speech. This framework just gives you one way to organize your ideas while you're being spontaneous and following a group conversation where it leads. Again, be sure to check out the next chapter for an even more spontaneous way to interact with a group.

AN EXAMPLE PROFESSIONAL ENTHUSIASM INTRODUCTION

If you're in a more formal professional context, or if someone directly asks "What do you do?" or "Tell me about yourself," this is the right time to focus on work.

If you're speaking with corporate representatives, recruiters, or other people who stand to directly impact the trajectory of your career, you will want to be sure you're ready to introduce yourself as a professional. But even though you're focused on work, the same rule of enthusiasm applies.

Choose an aspect of your work that you love (like helping businesses streamline processes, analyzing data to discover innovative solutions to challenging problems, or connecting better with consumers through social media) and let the listeners know how that aspect of your work has gone in the past, what you're working on now, and how you hope to expand on it in the future.

Create a few different ways to talk about your professional experience in a way that inspires you, and you'll be ready to talk to anyone.

Here are two examples (notice that the past, present, and future can come in any order):

Sarah

Present: I've been an engineer since college, and I really love breaking down different problems and using technology to solve them.

Past: It's been very rewarding to see my work make a real impact. In fact, on my last project, I examined a surgical device designed specifically for newborn babies and discovered a way to make it more flexible and consistent, leading to 20% reduction in patient mortality.

Future: In my next job, I want to join a top consultancy and help find solutions to healthcare problems at a much higher level across the industry.

Amit

Past: During my consulting years, I realized that the experiences I most valued were those that allowed me to help build something new. So I joined STARTCO, where I helped launch new products for a year before I started business school. The coolest product I helped launch is called a 'widget.' In only six months, we got it designed, manufactured, and distributed to a small market in Southern California.

Present: I'm currently here at SCHOOL to gain marketing expertise and general management skills because . . .

Future: My goal after business school is to transition into a product management role at a larger company. I have so much more to learn, and I hope to get some good training and mentoring in the nuances of customer insights in my next job.

WHAT IF YOU AREN'T 100% SURE ABOUT WHAT YOU WANT IN THE FUTURE?

Don't worry, you're not alone. The question: "What do I want to be when I grow up?" is one you will probably continue asking until you retire. Each new experience gives you more information about your values and passions and changes the opportunity set, requiring you to reconsider the future at each step.

Especially if you're at a career crossroads such as business school or a career transition, the entire world of opportunities available to you might be too exciting to nail it down to just one path.

That means you might want to have a plan to customize your introduction for each person you speak with. In fact, if you use the framework right, you'll never introduce yourself exactly the same way twice. And that's because . . .

GOOD COMMUNICATION HAPPENS HERE

What I know and want

What you know and want

For your introduction to really connect with the person you're speaking with, it needs to take into account what they want (in the case of recruiters: to hire passionate and inspiring people who have an interest in the work of their firm) and what they know (likely very little about your past industry, company, or role) while still allowing you to be spontaneous.

Notice how both Sarah and Amit kept the details to a high level anyone could understand. Sarah didn't talk about the software she used to design the device, the raw materials that went into it, or the specific data behind patient mortality. Likewise, Amit didn't get deep into product launch and customer marketing strategies. This is because most people wouldn't be able to follow such detailed accounts of your experience in a casual conversation at a networking event.

Keep this in mind when talking about the future, but be careful not to take this piece of advice into transaction territory. If you find yourself telling people why you want to work for their company before you're sure you actually do want to work for their company, then you're still trying to do a transaction.

Ultimately, all firms want to hire passionate and driven people who have a vested personal interest in learning and doing good work. So instead of pandering, talk about what's in it for you in terms of what they offer.

LET'S CONSIDER AN EXAMPLE

Here are two different ways the same person might introduce herself. Let's call her Vanessa. Imagine Vanessa is in business school right now, so she's in an active job search for her next role. Let's also imagine she's speaking to two different people at different times in the evening, both of whom work for companies she would like to form connections with:

1. A Senior Manager at Nike Corporate Strategy.

2. A Principal at a major consulting firm.

Introduction 1 (For Nike)

Past: What I love most about my work is helping solve customer issues and improving their lives. Before my MBA, I worked in a wearable technology company in the customer success division. My work involved strategizing better ways to meet customer needs.

Present: I came to business school so that I could learn more about both marketing and strategy to transition into a more impactful role in my field.

Future: In the long term, I hope to lead my own team within a larger organization and design customer success strategies for the whole company, and Nike would be an ideal place to launch the next phase of my career.

Introduction 2 (For Consulting)

Past: Before coming to business school, I worked in a wearable technology company in the customer success division, developing strategies and tactics that helped the company better meet customer needs.

Present: I'm in business school to learn more about marketing and strategy so that I can be successful running a much bigger team.

Future: I see consulting as a great next step to further train myself in strategy, business decision making, and project management while getting exposure to diverse customer success strategies across industries. Eventually I want to specialize in helping companies solve customer problems to improve their lives.

Notice how, in the second example, Vanessa expresses her interest in consulting without overreaching. She says why that job would be meaningful to her without declaring her undying commitment to the field, which at this point for her would be false. This kind of honesty and enthusiasm will naturally resonate with recruiters because someone who is personally interested in "training myself in strategy, business decision making, and project management" will naturally benefit from and contribute to the work and culture of a consulting firm. Vanessa made a connection without trying to make it a transaction.

With just these few examples, you can see that this simple framework allows you to improvise an infinite number of concise personal introductions to strangers that intrigue and inspire. Leveraging enthusiasm, your personal values will shine through, making a genuine connection.

So save the Elevator Pitch for your next big business idea, and instead, have fun with this framework!! With just a little practice, your self-confidence will grow, and you will soon effortlessly be making genuine connections using the power of spontaneity and enthusiasm.

A WORD ABOUT TIMING

It's important to have good timing when you introduce yourself at networking events. The right time to give a personal introduction like the ones we outlined above is when you have permission or an invitation to do so. Times such as . . .

- When someone asks what you do

- When everyone else in your conversation group is doing so, or

- When you have a moment 1:1 with someone

Even though an Enthusiasm Introduction works better than a traditional Elevator Pitch, it will still create an awkward moment if you do it at the wrong time.

Remember, because this isn't a true Elevator Pitch, you shouldn't be interrupting someone. If you're interrupting a conversation about a different topic that's already unfolding, you're making a mistake. That's bad timing.

Read the next chapter for an understanding of small talk and how to participate in a lively dialogue. Read Chapter 7 to learn how to enter a conversation and find your place among several other people who are already talking.

If you do these two things well, your moment to introduce yourself fully will come. And you can trust your common sense about the right timing.

NOT SURE WHAT TO TALK ABOUT AT NETWORKING EVENTS?

06

ARE YOU INSECURE ABOUT/TERRIBLE AT/UNINTERESTED IN SMALL TALK?

Me too. As an introvert and a relatively private person, there's nothing I used to dread more than standing in a crowd of people, trying to maintain interest in conversations I ultimately found boring.

But small talk doesn't have to be terrifying/awkward/torturous!! You will be doing everyone at the networking event a favor if you follow the tips in this chapter and lead the conversation to areas of intrigue and inspiration.

Once you're confident that you can introduce yourself with enthusiasm and spontaneity, you're going to be much more excited to get out there and mix it up.

But here are some questions you might have next:

• Apart from introducing myself, what should I talk about?

• Do I need to talk about work?

• How can I find a common interest with someone?

Remember, your job is to connect, not sell yourself. We're still in the initial connection stage of genuine friendship. You're trying to create a connection from one human being to another. Human beings are complex and multifaceted. So that means you don't have to talk about work! You can and you will talk about work. Your career is a big and important part of your life, so it's only natural that it'll be a topic of conversation. But it doesn't have to be.

That's the first thing to know. Even at a formal corporate meet and greet, the conversation doesn't have to focus on work, so you should feel free to discuss topics that interest you and follow the dialogue where it goes. And remember, this is not the time to try to stand out, grandstand, or make an elaborate personal introduction.

Finding a specific common interest with someone is a great way to make that important connection. When you find someone who shares your love of foreign cinema, Ethiopian food, or CrossFit, someone who grew up in your hometown, or someone who knows your best friend from college, you know you'll have a lot to talk about, and creating a future will be easy.

BUT FINDING A COMMON INTEREST CAN FEEL LIKE SEARCHING FOR A NEEDLE IN A HAYSTACK

You can't just run through the laundry list of your interests and hope for a match. And that's the wrong approach anyway; we're back to transactions, trying to find the magic key to unlock what we want.

The best way to start a friendship is just by being yourself. And that means, talking about stuff that's interesting and important to you. The irony of this approach is that leading with what you love will also help you find a common interest with absolutely everyone.

That's because one thing we all have in common is that we all want to feel more alive. Enthusiasm is a simple thing. It is both irresistible and contagious. When you discuss topics that make you come alive, then everyone else will come a little more alive too. It's a great feeling.

When you share a passion, you're inviting others to do the same. And even when you don't have a specific passion in common, you both love to love things, so you'll form a connection because you both had the chance to share something you love.

"One thing we all have in common is that
we all want to feel more alive."

The best topics of conversation at a networking event follow the principle of enthusiasm, just like your personal introduction. And the good news is, if you did the work in the last chapter, you're already halfway there!!

MASTERING SMALL TALK IS EASY!
JUST FOLLOW YOUR ENTHUSIASM!!

Talk about stuff you are enthusiastic about. That includes:

Stuff you love   Stuff you're curious about

Stuff that matters   Stuff you want

Because connection happens in the present moment, it's a good idea to come to a networking event with some topics of enthusiasm handy. But don't stop with a short list of things you love, think about what is happening or new in those areas right now, so that you have something fresh and inspiring to talk about.

Here are some examples of what I mean:

- Something you love: If you're a lover of food trucks, what was the best food truck you tried this month?

- Something that matters to you: If you volunteer for an organization that provides career support to the homeless, what new event has happened in the last few months that has helped fulfill organizational objectives?

- Something you're curious about: If you're just learning about corporate financial valuation, what is the big topic you're obsessed with learning about this week?

- Something you want: If you're in an active job search, what have you learned this week about your ideal target company and your own personal values through your research?

Here's a quick exercise you can do to make sure you're ready to go with new topics of discussion.

6.1 What's New?

Take your enthusiasm lists from chapter 5 and make a quick note of recent developments in those areas.

Here is what that might look like:

ENTHUSIASM	WHATS NEW?
Cooking	These days I am obsessed with fried things: meatballs, veggie balls, zucchini flowers, mushrooms, etc. I invented these quinoa veggie meatless balls that all my vegetarian friends love.
Food trucks	Just last month I finally got to try the famous Veracruz All-Natural Taco Truck in Austin, TX! Their migas is famous, but I have to admit I preferred the steak.

ENTHUSIASM	WHATS NEW?
Travel	I finally got to visit Dublin this spring and I loved it! The town had such an incredible energy—the tech scene is booming but it still has its old Irish charm.
Explaining complicated concepts in a simple way	Just last month I published a huge new blog post about an MBA Resume, where I broke down a brilliant bullet according to 3 different frameworks that make it easy to build one yourself! You can check it out here: http://careerprotocol.com/mba-resume/

You don't necessarily need to take such detailed notes. And DEFINITELY do not try to memorize a series of short What's New Speeches. Just take a moment before an event to reflect on what's new in your life so that these topics are top of mind for discussion.

"Conversation about the weather is
the last refuge of the unimaginative."

—OSCAR WILDE

DON'T KNOW HOW TO BUTT IN POLITELY?

07

NOW YOU KNOW WHAT TO TALK ABOUT, BUT HOW DO YOU EDGE YOUR WAY INTO A CONVERSATION THAT'S ALREADY UNDERWAY?

Let's say you find someone you want to talk to. Perhaps it's someone who works at a company where you're interviewing or someone who works at a school to which you're applying. The person is—not surprisingly—surrounded by other people, and everyone is talking.

Here are the questions you're probably asking:

- How do I get in there?

- How do I become a part of the conversation?

- How can I get their attention without seeming rude or intrusive?

The easiest way to enter a conversation already in progress is to be introduced. If you already know people in the room, use those relationships to your advantage. Ask them to connect you to others they know and return the favor. This is step 4 in the anatomy of a friendship anyway!!

But what if you're there alone? Or what if you don't know anyone who knows the person you want to talk to?

ONE EASY WAY TO ENTER ANY CONVERSATION ALREADY IN PROGRESS IS BY LISTENING

Most people don't fully understand the power of authentic listening to build human connections. The best way to listen when you're meeting strangers for the first time is with this question in mind: what is this person enthusiastic about? What makes them come alive?

Seeking to understand what lights a person up is a surefire way to make a connection.

Here's how to do it:

1. Join a group that's already speaking. If there's a brief pause in the conversation, say "Hi," or tell the person or the group next to you your name and company or school. (Note: DO NOT use your Enthusiasm Introduction here. It's not time yet!) If there's no conversational pause, just smile and nod. Be there, be comfortable, but don't speak.

2. Listen to the person who has the floor. Ask yourself this question: given what he or she is saying, what is this person really passionate about?

3. When there is a natural pause, ask the person speaking a question that allows him or her to expand on a passion.

4. Actually listen to what the person says.

Let's take an example here.

Imagine Julie is talking about a trip she took to Vietnam with her sister. She's describing a beautiful beach they visited that was very secluded and peaceful. She's brimming with enthusiasm. You can see that at least some of the things she cares about are family (or at least her relationship with her sister), travel, interacting with nature, and the experience of solitude and quiet. Here are some questions you could ask her:

- It sounds like you've found some beautiful places in your travels. What other places have you discovered?

- If you could recommend the three best things to do in Vietnam, what would they be?

- Do you get to travel often? Where else have you been?

- I'm curious if you have any good ideas for creating a feeling of peace and solitude here in the midst of work and the city. It's so wonderful to travel, but the challenge is bringing that feeling home. What do you think?

Notice how all of these questions are completely open-ended, allow Julie to expand on her experience and something she loves, and maintain a level of social distance that doesn't encroach into her personal life. For example, "What does your sister do?" "How did you afford that trip?" and "What does your family think about you taking a vacation with your sister?" would be too personal and inappropriate. (See Chapter 8 for more about safe social distance.)

Notice also that these suggested questions focus on Julie and her experience and don't attempt to deflect attention off of her and onto you. Here are some examples that would do that:

- "Oh, I've been to Vietnam too! My favorite place was . . . "

- "You know, my favorite nature spot is . . . "

- "Have you been to the beach in Bali? It's amazing because . . . "

There's a proper time to introduce your own ideas into the conversation, and it will soon be your turn to share your own experiences. But as it turns out, listening first makes a better impression—it respects the people who are already conversing, shows that you have a sense of humility and an interest in others, and enables the speaker to share his or her enthusiasm, which is an experience we all love to have.

"Listening makes the best first impression."

This is connection dynamite. When people feel heard and appreciated, they can't help but feel connected. This is what you give them when you actually listen and then ask thoughtful questions.

SPECIAL TIP FOR INTROVERTS

———

Listening to and connecting with others through what they say likely comes very naturally to you. Use this ability to listen to and understand others to build meaningful connections even if you are surrounded by a crowd of people!!!

So don't forget the last and most important step: Actually listen to what the person says. People know when you aren't listening. They can tell when you're just waiting to talk. If you don't listen, you'll destroy all the goodwill you created by asking such an interesting question and the connection will disintegrate. So listen, pay attention, and follow the conversation wherever it goes!

Soon enough the conversation will turn to you, and you'll know what to do.

WORRIED YOU'LL EMBARRASS YOURSELF OR SOMEONE ELSE WHILE NETWORKING?

08

NO ONE WANTS TO STEP ON TOES, MAKE PEOPLE UNCOMFORTABLE, OR CROSS SOCIAL BOUNDARIES WHEN THEY FIRST MEET SOMEONE

So far, we've covered the three major kinds of communication you'll have when getting to know people for the first time:

1. Introducing yourself when the time is right.

2. Mastering small talk and discussing broader topics that interest you.

3. Listening to others and asking thoughtful questions that let them share their enthusiasm.

As you're strategizing, brainstorming, and practicing the first two, trust yourself in choosing topics.

Generally speaking, topics that relate to sex and other bodily functions would be inappropriate in any professional setting, but I don't have to tell you that, right? Apart from those topics, when you're talking about yourself and your experience, your favorite subjects should work.

But when the conversation turns to others, you need to be mindful of social distance. Social distance tells us where people draw the lines of privacy, and therefore what's OK to ask about. The closer the relationship, and the more trust that exists, the more topics of conversation are available to you. This is why there are certain things about you that only a sibling, a parent, or significant other knows. Those are the people with whom you have the least social distance.

Strangers stand at the greatest social distance. So you need to respect the lines of privacy when asking them questions. Another way to think about this is that there are certain topics you just shouldn't ask about until you have permission or an invitation to do so.

Understanding social distance and taking a conservative approach is especially important if you're networking in a culture different from your own.

LET ME ILLUSTRATE THE IMPORTANCE OF SOCIAL DISTANCE WITH A STORY

I lived in South Korea in my 20s. At first, I was too poor to take taxis. But eventually, I had both the language skills and the disposable income to occasionally indulge in what we affectionately called the "Seoul Bullet Taxis." (Bullet, not because of their steely color, but because they flew like hot, crazy lead through the tangle of perpetual Seoul gridlock.)

Almost every time, it was the same. I'd get in and tell them where I was going.

"Where are you from?" they'd ask. In those days, there weren't a lot of expats in the Hermit Kingdom, so on many occasions, I was the first foreigner the driver was meeting. And I was certainly the first Korean-speaking foreigner many of them had met. Can you guess what the second question Korean cabbies would ask me after I told them where I was from?

"How old are you?"

The third question?

"Are you married?"

When I said no, typically a lengthy debate ensued about why not, and how I was getting up there in years (I was 24) and so I'd better hurry, and maybe I should find a Korean husband.

The typical fourth question, if you can believe it, and if we managed to get past this marriage argument, was typically, "How much money do you make?"

Now, most Americans, and particularly, most American women, would probably have been deeply offended by each and every one of these questions. By the time I started encountering such cross-examination from strangers, I had been in Korea long enough to understand that their cultural norms about personal information varied radically from those I grew up with. Questions about age, marital status, and income were actually par for the course in Korean culture.

There's a good reason for that. Their social structure is driven by hierarchical relationships—even the very structure of the language is founded on this hierarchy. Verb conjugations change depending on the relative age of the person you're talking to, so in order to even know how to address me, someone I met needed to know if I was older or younger than him.

Korean cultural norms are built on the nuclear family and the surrounding community. So matters of relationship status and income were not private facts in those days. It was considered totally acceptable to ask a relative stranger how much money they made.

Like I said, fortunately, I had figured this out by the time I encountered it en masse.

But imagine, for a moment, one of those Korean cabbies trying to network in America. Imagine someone whose social norms dictate that they first need to establish someone's age and social status in an overt way before getting to know them better. Now imagine him trying to navigate a culture where those details are actually the most private and personal details about you. (I mean, if you live in America, even your closest friends probably don't know how much money you make!)

Yeah, it's a recipe for disaster.

WHAT DOES THIS MEAN FOR YOU?

If you've never been in the position of needing to connect with members of a different culture, hopefully it at least gives you a little more compassion for the challenge immigrants and international business people face on a daily basis, engaging in the most fundamental of human tasks—building relationships.

The point here is that we've all been rubbed the wrong way by a question. We've all encountered people we thought were rude. We all inherently know the pitfalls and no one wants to be the persona non grata. But knowing that it's possible to be that way even by mistake might cast your actions into doubt and make you feel like you have to tip toe and "watch yourself" at networking events.

No one likes to self-censor. It's stifling. It's going to be a lot harder to enjoy networking events if you feel like you're treading a conversational minefield with a blindfold on.

SO LET'S TAKE THE BLINDFOLD OFF

Although every individual has his or her own boundaries, we tend to conform to the expectations of our culture. Cultural norms vary widely. In some countries, as my story illustrates, it's fine to bring up salary, marital status, family, or age in a first conversation. In others, these subjects are strictly taboo.

I'm American, and the American concept of social distance seems to be the most conservative, so I recommend following American norms about social distance when meeting someone for the very first time. If you're in doubt about which topics are safe to discuss and ask about, respect this Social Distance Circle. Stay in the outer circle!

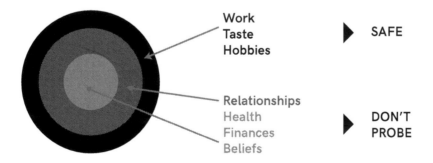

The Social Distance Circle is an easy framework for understanding the boundaries of personal privacy in American culture. In the United States, people hold their bodies, personal health, finances, and beliefs most sacred and personal. So it would generally be considered inappropriate to discuss body issues, income, religion, spirituality, and politics with someone you just met. These are subjects you want to avoid discussing unless someone else invites a conversation about them. And even then, proceed with extreme caution. When in doubt, move the conversation to an outer circle topic.

Likewise, you shouldn't inquire about someone's marital or parental status—their relationships. Wait until someone else brings up those subjects before discussing them. This doesn't mean you can't mention your significant other or kids in a conversation, it just means that to be as conservative as possible, you shouldn't ask about the relationship status of others. Let them bring it up.

THE TOPICS THAT ARE GENERALLY SAFE TO INITIATE AND INQUIRE ABOUT ARE WORK, HOBBIES, AND TASTES

———

Most people enjoy discussing food, films, and fun, for example. Asking about the nature of someone's work and pastimes is also a great place to start. But for the more inner circles of social distance, it's best to allow the other person to broach the subject and invite a discussion about it before you inquire.

If the dividing lines aren't clear, be conservative and focus the conversation on pastimes—activities that you do.

Take the example of vegan cuisine. You might be passionate about eating vegan for a variety of reasons. At a networking event, you can freely share your favorite recipes and restaurants. But if you start talking about your belief that eating meat is wrong, you've moved into the inner circle. You're risking crossing a social boundary, sparking an uncomfortable debate, or alienating someone you're trying to connect with.

Debating opinions and challenging beliefs is a great way to DEEP-EN a connection, but it's not the best way to start one. That's because conversations about beliefs and other inner circle topics require an open mind, a suspension of judgment, and a willingness to be vulnerable and disagree peacefully. Humans create these conditions much more readily when there is already a sufficient foundation of trust—a foundation that's unlikely to develop in a first meeting.

Save the debates, challenging conversations, and sensitive subjects for later, once you've developed a genuine friendship.

BUT AT A NETWORKING EVENT, ESPECIALLY WHEN YOU'RE ASKING QUESTIONS OF OTHERS, STEER CLEAR OF THE INNER CIRCLE TOPICS.

———

When in doubt, respect social distance. The most conservative conversational topics are tastes, work, and hobbies. If you're worried about crossing lines and embarrassing others or yourself, stick to those subjects and you can't go wrong.

TOP TIP

———

Pay attention to positive emotion. Follow up on or initiate any topic of conversation that elevates your mood and that of others. Positive emotion lends itself to more positive connections with others.

8.1 Social Distance Exercise

As a quick check before a networking event, take a look at your enthusiasm lists. Decide which topics, if any, risk creeping into the inner circles of social distance.

Here are a few examples for illustration:

- Dating

- The elections (I know it's so hard to resist, but try!)

- Death and the afterlife

- Fertility, pregnancy, childbirth, parenting strategies

- Ongoing health problems (the cold you had last week is probably ok, but, ya know, probably not something you're enthusiastic about!)

- Weight and weight loss

- The cost of important things (rent, mortgage, daycare, student loans are off limits; restaurants, those shoes you bought on sale, trivial things are probably OK)

The list could go on. Most of us have passions that touch on the very inner part of the social distance circle. You should certainly never inquire about these topics at a networking event. And if you want to be conservative, plan not to bring them up. Plan to discuss them later: only once you feel you've established a connection with someone.

Here is a quick example of what this might look like in practice:

One of my favorite topics of conversation is dating and relationships. I'm frequently the person my friends come to for advice about these subjects. Since I'm a student of human nature, you might imagine that I find online dating fascinating. It sometimes happens that other people talk about being single and about the various ways they're trying to remedy that at a networking event. When that happens, I feel safe to dive right in and share my own insights. But I try never to bring the topic of dating up myself.

I met Hanna at a networking event. When we first met, we talked about our jobs. We then connected via email. When I was in her town next, I sent her a message and we attended another networking event together where we discussed work again. In between we had a phone call, where we talked about a work project we were considering doing together.

Finally—in our fourth meeting—we met alone for coffee and dug into our personal lives. We compared notes about our experiences dating and shared war stories. It was this conversation that turned us from professional associates into friends. We still talk about work more than our personal lives, but now we also consider each other friends: we've crossed into the innermost circle of social distance.

In the case of Hanna and me, we weren't ready to go there until our fourth conversation. Sometimes, people will invite you into their inner circles sooner. Some people will never invite you in. The important thing to keep in mind is the invitation. Wait until you are invited into a discussion about inner circle topics. At a networking event, wait until you have the other person's tacit permission by virtue of the fact that they initiate the discussion before you proceed into the inner circles.

If you respect this "rule," you should be able to engage in small talk with great confidence, no matter what culture you come from.

A FEW CLOSING WORDS
ABOUT SOCIAL DISTANCE

I'd love it if you would use this chapter as a guard rail—as a set of training wheels. When it comes to genuine human connection, at bottom, there really are no rules. Each new connection transpires spontaneously in its own time, and no two human connections are exactly the same. That means that it's entirely possible to create an awesome relationship with someone with a conversation that races right to the inner circle of social distance in the first 30 seconds.

If you have an approach to social distance you're already comfortable with, don't fix what ain't broke!! On the other hand, if you find yourself wondering if and when you might offend people, then use this chapter not as a prescription. Use it as a framework to play with so that you can discover the natural boundaries that work best for you in each different situation.

After many years of teaching this stuff, I can trust myself to go just about anywhere in a first conversation without worrying about offending someone. I can trust myself to read the dynamic to know what might make someone uncomfortable and how to phrase questions in an inoffensive way. I make spontaneous choices about what to talk about. But it took me a long time and a lot of trial and error to really feel fully comfortable with that strategy.

So use the "rules" of social distance to the extent that they make you feel more confident. Consider the Social Distance Circle a map to where conversational mines (if there are any) are most likely to be. Steer clear of them, or try to blow one up every now and again and see what happens. Have fun with it, but let respect for other people be your guiding intention.

All great connections rest on a foundation of mutual respect.

DO YOUR NEW NETWORKING CONTACTS FALL OFF A CLIFF?

09

YOU MET, YOU TALKED, AND
IT WAS GREAT! NOW WHAT?

If you implement the ideas in the previous chapters, you're off to an amazing start to professional friendships: you're making genuine connections that feel good and make networking fun.

Let's imagine you made a connection at a networking event with Jacob. The two of you talked for ten minutes about your shared interests in golf and French cheese. The night ended. You said goodbye and went home without knowing how to contact him. Or—potentially even worse—you got his business card but didn't create any context for follow-up.

The evening yielded a nice conversation, but the relationship has no future. That means, Jacob is not going to become a professional friend.

THE CONNECTION EXPIRED BECAUSE
YOU DIDN'T GIVE IT A FUTURE.

Part of successful networking involves staying in the present moment and making the most of it, it means listening to others, and it means being yourself and creating a meaningful connection. But all of that will be for naught if the connection doesn't survive beyond your first contact.

Giving the connection a future is the easiest part of the networking process and the simplest thing to do, but it also causes a lot of anxiety for people.

Questions you probably have as you're conversing with someone you feel connected to:

1. How do I end this conversation gracefully and move onto others?

2. How do I get his card without seeming grabby or like I'm trying to use him?

3. Even if I do get his card, then what?

If you feel nervous at this point in the conversation, you're still operating in the transaction paradigm of networking.

It's completely natural to ask someone for their contact information if you made a connection. It doesn't obligate them to give you a job or to do you any favors of any kind. It also doesn't obligate you to ask for a job or a favor. It simply enables the relationship to have a future. And without a future, the relationship does not exist.

It's very easy to create a future for any connection. You just need two things.

| A way to contact them | A context for the next step | A Future |

Of course, you need his or her contact information (LinkedIn profile, email, phone number, business card, whatever method you prefer). But that's not enough. You also need a reason and the person's permission to follow up. You need a specific context for the next step.

The best way to do this is to stick to something that keeps the conversation going on the path it started.

Did you discuss the local restaurant scene? Propose lunch at your favorite spot or promise to send a list of your top 5 dinner restaurants.

Did you discuss someone's work? Ask them if you can follow up and do an informational interview (see Chapter 11).

The possibilities are endless. But in case you need more creative inspiration, here are 14 ways to end a conversation and create a future.

Ask for something:

1. I'd love to speak with you for 15 minutes about your work. I'll reach out to schedule a call!

2. I can't wait to read the article you told me about. I'll shoot you an email tomorrow so you can forward it to me.

3. Could I have your card? I'd love to follow up with you about the culture of your firm.

4. You seem to be an expert on the local restaurant scene. Would it be OK if I email you later this week for some recommendations?

5. Your personal trainer sounds amazing, could I ping you Tuesday to get her contact info?

6. I've been trying to learn more about social media, and you seem to be really knowledgeable about it. Would you be open to a 20-minute coffee chat next week?

7. I'm going to connect with you on LinkedIn so that we can keep talking about TOPIC WE DISCUSSED.

Offer something:

1. Let me know your email and I'll forward you the article we spoke about!

2. I'd love to introduce you to my friend who's interested in working for your company.

3. I'll be back in the San Francisco area in March, so let me take you out to lunch.

4. I'd be happy to share my top 5 travel tips for Thailand for your upcoming trip!

5. I don't think we're connected on LinkedIn, but if you'll add me, I'll connect you with my friend who works at the company you're interviewing with next week.

6. I need to look up the name of that restaurant, but I'll send it to you next week. Give me your email address.

7. If you'll give me your email, I'll follow up after my project and share my top insights with you.

Just be sure to create a specific next step as you get their card. Something as simple as "I'd love to follow up with you and talk more about TOPIC YOU DISCUSSED. Could I email you next week?" works!!

TOP TIP

———

Create a next step you're excited about so you're sharing and connecting based on what you love!

AS WITH ALL THINGS, DON'T FORCE IT

The more specific and grounded in a real action you can make it, the better. But if during the conversation, you can't think of a single specific next step to give your connection a future, then just keep it simple: "I would really love to stay in touch. Would you mind if I reach out to you in the next few weeks?" If your connection agrees, then follow up in whatever way seems natural.

Please note though: the more tangible the follow up is (as in the list of asks and offers above) the easier it will be for you to follow up and for them to respond. You will have bounded the actions to something specific and it's always easier to take a specific action (send an article) than a general one (follow up). So do your best to find a specific reason to follow-up that flows naturally from where the connection started.

You won't follow up with everyone you meet. You won't turn every single "hello" into a professional friendship. If you're setting goals, making one genuine connection per event would be a fantastic outcome.

But for each person you DO want to develop a friendship with, make sure he or she is EXPECTING to receive a follow-up from you (or has promised to follow up with you), ideally on a concrete topic: an article, a referral, or a specific follow-up opportunity or conversation.

DO YOU FORGET TO FOLLOW UP?

10

DO NOT SKIP THIS STEP!!!

You made a connection.

You got their card.

You created a future—a specific next step.

The only thing you have to do now is follow through.

It's surprising how many times we humans go wrong here. We're busy, we forget, and by the time we get around to it, it seems like it's too late, so we never actually follow up.

But once you've given the connection a future and created a reason to follow up with the person, you need to do just that: follow up!

That very first follow-up is absolutely critical. Here are some tips to help you make the transition successfully from networking contact to budding professional friendship via a powerful first follow-up.

Do It Right Away. Human connections have a momentum all their own. You met someone at a networking event on Tuesday, got his or her business card, and offered to email an article you discussed. Unless you promised to do so next week, or in June, for example, consider sending the email Tuesday night before you go to bed, on Wednesday morning, or on Thursday at the latest. The longer you wait to follow up, the less likely you are to do it in the first place, and the less likely you are to receive a response. So for the most important people you meet, follow up right away or on the specific timeline you indicated when you met.

Keep Your Word. Did you promise to introduce Jiyoung to your friend who works at Google? Did you say you would invite Hector out for coffee at a new place you just discovered? Did you tell

Jonathan you would send him an article from *The Atlantic* about a passion you share? Do it. Plain and simple, do what you said.

Keep It Brief and Personal. People are busy. So in your follow-up email, LinkedIn request, or Facebook message, be sure to stick to the basics. Say what a pleasure it was to meet him or her. Follow up on your question or the offer you discussed. And then sign off. A follow-up communication doesn't usually require more than a few lines.

Following up and doing what you said when you said you would is the first step to keeping the relationship moving forward. But remember,

IF THE RELATIONSHIP HAS NO FUTURE, IT'S NOT A RELATIONSHIP

———

This means you're going to have to keep the relationship moving forward at every step until a true friendship blossoms.

In any conversation with a professional contact you haven't known for very long, it's a good idea to create the next opportunity for follow-up. Some ideas . . .

Make an Ask: "I would really appreciate if I could follow up with you in the next few months to see if you have any openings on your team. Would that be okay? And if you do think of a position that would be a good fit for me, please let me know."

Make an Offer: "I read an article last week that reminded me of the challenges you described in your job. I'll send it to you when I get back to my office."

Make an Introduction: "I have a friend who's job searching right now who would be very interested in the opportunity you described. I'll put you in touch."

Simply Promise to Follow Up: "I'd love to follow up with you and keep you posted on my progress as I go through recruiting. I will be in touch again in the coming months."

THEN MAKE SURE YOU ACTUALLY FOLLOW UP AS YOU PROMISED AND REPEAT THE CYCLE!

———

Especially if the new connection you've made is someone senior to you, you can expect to carry the majority of the burden of keeping the relationship alive for many of the first steps. This means you can't be afraid to keep following up multiple times. That's how the relationship moves forward!! It doesn't always have to be an ask or an offer; sometimes the best way to keep things moving forward is just to stay in touch. As long as you're appreciative and polite, you don't need to worry about being perceived as pushy or rude.

Let's take an example.

You met Jorge at a networking event. He works at a tech start-up. In your follow-up email exchange, you let him know you were interested in working for a big tech company and he introduced you to Hasan, who works for one of the tech giants.

You had a great informational interview with Hasan and sent Jorge an update, thanking him again for introducing you.

But don't stop there.

After a few weeks, follow up with Jorge again.

Try something like this:

Hi Jorge!

Thanks again for the introduction to Hasan! As you know, I'm seeking a position in the marketing department of a large tech firm. This week, I'm interviewing with Cisco for a second time. I'm told I could have ten more interviews before I may or may not get an offer, so we'll see how it goes! Anyway, I just wanted to thank you for your support and encouragement again and let you know that I'm still plugging away. No need to reply to this email! I will reach out again when I have more news.

Best, Jenny

The purpose of this email is simply to express appreciation and keep in touch.

Notice Jenny isn't asking for anything. She very well could have, but given that Jorge is still a relative stranger who probably doesn't know much about how things work at Cisco, she's just keeping the relationship moving forward without placing any burden on him.

If Jorge happens to know someone at Cisco and wants to put in a good word for her, that's his choice. If he interviewed there and has some insight to share, he can do that too. But that's up to him.

Notice how Jenny even lets Jorge off the hook for following up! This makes his life very easy. He'll be happy to get her message, happy to spend 10 seconds reading and archiving it, and happy that he knows that he needs to do exactly nothing to keep the relationship moving forward. This is useful when building friendships with busy people. When the time comes to really ask them a favor, they will be much more likely to say yes because you've kept in touch, expressed appreciation, and made it easy for them to respond to your communications.

Regardless of how Jorge responds to this email, Jenny's next step is to. . . . guess what . . . ? Keep the relationship moving forward!

- She can follow up and let him know how her interviews at Cisco went.

- She can make sure he knows when she gets the job.

- She can let him know about the next opportunity she's pursuing.

- She can make another concrete ask: for a new connection, for a referral, for a recommendation.

- And of course, she can always follow up with resources that might be useful to him: articles, contacts, information.

Professional friendships are just like personal ones: they blossom and deepen over time and through consistent communication. So don't be shy. Decide on an appropriate follow-up frequency for those in your network, and then communicate with your connections based on that schedule.

When you're not in an active job search, every few months should suffice for most connections. For some, even once a year is enough. But always create a next step, keep it brief and personal, and keep the connection moving forward. This way the relationship will always have a future, and voilà, soon you have a professional friendship!

TOP TIP

Integrity is the foundation of trust. When communicating with new connections, always do *what* you said you would do *when* you said you would do it.

> ## 10.1 Take a moment to get back in touch
>
> Have some of your important connections gone cold? Take a moment to reach out and just say hello.
>
> Make a list of all the people who come to mind that you've been meaning to follow up with. Just write down everyone who comes to mind.
>
> Now go and drop each of them a quick "thinking about you" note. Use email, LinkedIn, Facebook messenger, whatever format most suits the way you usually communicate.
>
> For the next few weeks, as new people who you've lost touch with come to mind, just drop them a line as soon as you think of it.

If you want to download my thank you note and keep in touch template emails, you can get them here: careerprotocol.com/emails

MAKE A KEEP-IN-TOUCH PLAN

———

We're all busy. There's no question about it.

Despite its critical importance to our success and happiness, relationship building frequently creeps down our to-do list or even falls off. That's why it's best to have a plan, a process, and tools in place to make keeping in touch an easier, more integrated part of your life.

Whether you use a spreadsheet, a free web-based tool, or a paid service, be sure to have a way to track the frequency of your communication with key contacts.

NOT SURE HOW TO GET TO THE NEXT STEP WITH NETWORKING CONTACTS?

11

HERE'S AN EXCELLENT TOOL TO CREATE YOUR NEXT POSITIVE SHARED EXPERIENCE

It's called an Informational interview. It gives you the chance to learn by example from people who have become successful in your industry, people whose advice and experiences could help you on your career path. You can take an active role in your professional growth by asking someone you admire for an informational interview—someone in a firm you're interested in joining or a school you're thinking about applying to, for example.

An awesome informational interview is an indispensable tool for your career. It will help you to perform due diligence on firms that interest you, learn about potential job opportunities, and inform your goals. But most importantly for the purposes of this book, it is an easy and powerful way to deepen a professional friendship. Because you're giving the gift of unconditional listening to your new contact. That always feels good.

HERE'S WHY: EVERYONE LOVES TO TALK ABOUT THEIR EXPERIENCES AND GIVE ADVICE

It's a fact about human nature that our own experiences become more meaningful to us when we are invited to recount them to others. This is why storytelling is the oldest human art form—the one, some anthropologists believe, that gave rise to language in the first place. We just love to tell stories—or in other words—educate and entertain others with our own personal experiences.

A great informational interview gives your new contact the chance to do just that! And since work is on the outer circle of safe social distance, it's the ideal second conversation to have with anyone you meet networking.

So, when you create a future with someone, there are countless possible next steps, but one that will almost always work (especially for people senior to you) is an informational interview. It's when you sit them down (or get them on the phone) for 20 minutes, tell them a little about yourself, and then ask insightful questions about the company they work for and the work they do. If you do it right, you will not only gain valuable insider information, but you will also deepen your relationship with your new contact and open the door for next steps.

HERE IS MY 8-STEP PROCESS FOR CONDUCTING AN AWESOME INFORMATIONAL INTERVIEW

Get Introduced

You can skip this step if you already met them at a networking event. But if you're in an active job search, you may need to approach strangers and people you haven't met yet. If that's the case, ideally, you'll use your network to get connected directly to people who work in the firms you're interested in. When you're introduced to someone, it makes it much more likely that they'll agree to speak with you. Once someone has agreed to an informational interview, there are a few keys to remember to make the most out of your time.

Respect Their Time

Everyone is busy. So keep it brief. Ask for 20 minutes to talk. Recognize you may have to conform to their schedule so propose a few specific times and ask them to give you some alternatives if your proposed times don't work. The phone will work best for most people, so don't propose coffee or a live meeting unless you're confident they have the bandwidth. Then make sure you're ready to get everything you need in those 20 minutes. If they want to extend the conversation, that's up to them.

Do Your Research

Speaking directly with someone at a target firm is a rare opportunity for primary research. So don't ask basic questions that you could find on the internet. Especially if you are in a job search or if the firm is one you would consider working for, do your best to leverage publicly available information to ascertain things such as . . .

- Where the firm is located and whether it has offices in different geographies you are interested in

- The nature of the position you'd be interested in (e.g. entry level analyst, senior consultant, etc.)

- Any recent news coverage related to the company—earnings releases, mergers, changes in leadership, etc.

Even if you're not in an active job search or interested in the company, do your basic due diligence; visit the company website, read the LinkedIn description of your contact's job and role, check out any other relevant links on the first page of a Google search on the company name.

Know What They Have to Offer

Don't just research the firm. Also make sure to research the individual to whom you will be speaking. Use LinkedIn and the company website to familiarize yourself with your interviewee's basic information—title, tenure with the firm, career trajectory prior to this role, etc. This is critical to asking great questions.

The bulk of your conversation should focus on your new contact's own personal experiences. Even if you're looking for a job, this conversation isn't about you or your search. So you'll want to give the person ample time and space to discuss what they've learned and what they know. Focus on their experiences.

If you're in an active job search and do have specific questions to ask about the firm and available opportunities, save that for the last half of the conversation, and be sure to focus on what the person knows.

For example, if you think you'll be interested in a position in the finance department of this particular company, and your interviewer is on the marketing team, she might not know much about the challenges a finance associate will face. That said, she'll know plenty about corporate culture, firm success factors, and the interview process. Leverage the expertise of the person you're talking to and show respect for their time by asking them questions they can answer and that allow them to expand on their own experiences.

Set the Context

Do not neglect this step. Before you jump in and begin firing off questions, let the person know who you are. Introduce yourself briefly. The Enthusiasm Introduction in Chapter 5 is actually a great framework to use here!! Let them know the past, present and future about an aspect of your work that's meaningful to you and be sure to explain how that relates to their work and company if in fact you are looking for opportunities with their firm. People want to be useful to you, and you make it much easier for them to do that when you tell them what you want and need from the conversation.

Here's an example of how you might set the context:

> *Jane, thank you so much for taking time to speak with me today. Let me tell you a little bit about myself before we dig into the conversation. I got my MBA at Harvard, and in the past four years since I graduated, I've worked as a management consultant, conducting strategy projects for companies in the consumer goods industry. I quickly realized that not all companies are the same, and the projects that have always been the most fulfilling are those that involve not just profit impact, but also social impact. Now I'm looking to bring my strategy experience to bear for a company that has a dual bottom line,*

and I'm targeting a medium-sized firm with a socially responsible mission. I'm so excited to talk to you about your experiences at Warby Parker, because the company's business model really inspires me.

Ask Great Questions

Everyone likes to talk about their experience and most people like to give advice. These are also the two topics that will make your informational interview most valuable. It might even be worth your time to create an interview guide for your conversation. You'll get much more valuable information if you ask questions that require robust answers. So instead of vague questions such as "What is your job like?" consider asking ones that let the speaker go into detail more readily, such as "Describe what your work life looks like in a typical week."

Here are some topics to explore.

Their Past

- Tell me about your journey to work at firm X. How did you get here?

- What have been some of the most valuable lessons you've learned so far in your career?

- Tell me about the most meaningful project you've done.

- What would you say is the underlying passion behind the professional choices you've made?

- What advice do you have for someone starting out on their career journey?

The Work Itself

- What does a day or week in your life look like? What percent of your time do you spend in meetings, on email, on the phone, working on the computer, traveling, etc?

- What do you find most rewarding about your work?

- What problems have you been most passionate about solving?

- What aspects of the job have you struggled with most? What aspects of the (position I'm interested in) do people tend to struggle with most?

Firm Culture

- How would you characterize the culture of the firm?

- How do people collaborate and work together here?

- What values are emphasized in teamwork?

- What kind of people have not been great fits at this company?

- What would you suggest I do to learn more about the firm's culture?

Success Criteria

- On what key dimensions are you evaluated in your work? What key dimensions is the (position I'm interested in) evaluated on?

- What are the three core skills without which you could not have succeeded?

- What are the key development areas you're working on now?

- Do you have any advice for me on core skills or qualities to develop that would make me a better candidate for the position I'm interested in?

This isn't an exhaustive list. These are just a few ideas to get you thinking about what you want to know. Be sure to ask questions you're genuinely curious about.

And notice how most of the questions above center on the interviewee's own work and the "what" of the job. This enables the individual to expand on his or her own experiences rather than just giving opinions, which may or may not be relevant to your own job search.

It also opens the door for him or her to tell stories. And this is where your relationship will deepen and move to the next level, provided that you . . .

Listen

Listen. Listen to what they say. Listen—as you will do in networking conversations—to what makes them come alive. Ask follow-up questions that flow naturally from their answers. Be present. Take notes if you want, but genuinely listen. People know when you aren't listening—even over the phone!—and there is little more alienating than the feeling you are being ignored and disregarded.

Give the Connection a Future

Sound familiar? Ha! This is the important last step in any conversation. Create an opportunity for follow-up. This is as simple as asking for something or offering something.

For example . . .

- **An Ask:** I would really appreciate if I could follow up with you in the next several months to see if you have any openings on your team, would that be alright? And if you do think of a position that would be a good fit for me, please let me know.

- **An Offer:** I read an article last week that reminded me of the challenges you described in your job. I'll send it to you when I get back to my office.

Then make sure you actually follow up as you promised!

Use the informational interview liberally—when you're researching new jobs, actively searching for your next role, or when you'd just like to get to know someone and their work better. It's a great first or second step in developing professional friendships.

"I've learned that people will forget what you said, people will forget what you did, but people will never forget how you made them feel."

—MAYA ANGELOU

FEEL AWKWARD ASKING NEW CONTACTS FOR FAVORS?

12

HOW DO YOU KNOW WHEN IT'S OK TO MAKE A REQUEST OF A NEW CONTACT?

So far, I've discussed building new connections, giving the connections a future, following up, and keeping the relationship moving forward.

Throughout most of this process, you've placed your own agenda on hold. At some point, though, it may be time to make a request: to ask your new connection to do something for you.

Think about what it's like to ask a favor of an old friend. You probably already have a strong enough relationship and feel that you can ask for almost anything: help packing and moving across the country, an enthusiastic referral for a job interview, or a blind date fixup.

But what if the connection is still relatively new, the person is in a position to help with something you need now, and you want to make a request? How do you do so gracefully?

Here's an important fact about human nature that you already know, but probably forget from time to time.

People actually love to be of service.

Think about this from your own experience.

Remember a time that you gave someone else a piece of advice or helped them learn something new? Maybe you stayed late to help a colleague figure out a model, you gave your younger sibling college admissions advice, or you helped a stranger on the street find a store they were looking for. The example can be big or small, but think about a specific time you helped someone.

How did it feel?

Didn't it feel AWESOME?!!! Didn't it make you feel important, valued, meaningful, useful, smart, kind, generous, happy, ecstatic, open, amazed, gleeful, or any number of other great and uplifting feelings?

See, the thing about us humans, is that we actually LOVE to be of service to our fellow humans. It's hardwired in us. We get a genuine personal thrill out of contributing to other people's lives (success, happiness, etc.).

That means that asking someone to assist you with something they're able to provide can actually be a contribution to them too. The closer the friendship, the more you can ask for and the more they'll gladly give.

But for new connections, it's important not to overreach.

Trust your intuition. There are definitely times to make direct bold requests such as: "I'd love it if you would recommend me for this position in your company. Do you feel comfortable doing that?" If you believe that your new connection would endorse you enthusiastically, then try the direct approach.

But in most cases, if the contact is very new, following these three principles will feel better to you, and therefore likely lead to a better result.

KEEP THESE THREE PRINCIPLES IN MIND WHEN MAKING REQUESTS OF NEW CONNECTIONS:

---

1. Be appropriate.

This simply means don't ask for too much. You can ask your college roommate to help you move. You can ask a high school friend to dog-sit for the weekend. You can ask a long-time former colleague to interview you for a position on his new team. But asking these things of someone you just met would be inappropriate. Keep the request appropriate to the duration of your acquaintance and the level of friendship and trust you have established.

2. Be transparent.

That said, if what you ultimately want is a job opportunity with the company at which your connection works, don't hide your agenda. Include your aspirations as part of your request while still asking for something appropriate to your level of familiarity (like an informational interview or an introduction to a colleague in the team that's hiring).

3. Be willing to earn it.

If someone vouches for you within their own personal network, they suddenly bear a certain amount of reputational risk on your behalf. If you're asking someone to open a door for you, you must be willing to earn that opportunity and not expect a relative stranger to just hand it to you. This means that instead of asking for the opportunity itself, it might be better to ask for the chance to earn it.

Let's consider an example:

You met someone at a networking event last night. You want to work for her company. Although ideally you would've cultivated this connection over time—by maintaining communication, staying in touch, and adding value to her life—time is short. You know her company has an open position, and you want to be considered before it's too late.

Even if you had a very strong connection last night when you met, unless she specifically offered of her own accord to invite you to interview, or to recommend you for the job, or to introduce you directly to the person who's hiring for the position, it would probably feel uncomfortable to make a direct request of such a new connection.

If you know you're looking for a job right now, you might say something like:

"I'm excited to learn more about your company and to find out if I would be a good fit. Could I reach out to you tomorrow to schedule a quick follow-up conversation with you?"

This would be a really appropriate next step for a new connection.

But let's say you already had an informational interview with her and/or after your first follow-up conversation, you realize there's an open position at her firm that you're interested in. If you've created one or two positive interactions already, she should be predisposed to help you. Even though it's still early in the relationship, you could follow up with a request like one of the following:

"I really appreciate your time in speaking to me last week. I feel like I now have a really solid understanding of firm culture, and I'm all the more excited about the company. I noticed that the strategy team currently has an open position. I'd love to learn more about the role to find out if I would be a good fit. Is there someone on the team you could connect me with who might have 20 minutes to chat with me?"

Or

"I'm planning to apply for the strategy position that's currently open, and I wondered if you have any advice for me. I'd love the chance to speak directly to the appropriate person about my qualifications and see if I could add value to the role. Please let me know if you have any suggestions about the channels I should follow to connect with the right person."

Or

"I'm planning to submit my resume for the open strategy position, and I would love to talk with you just a bit more about the firm's culture before I apply. Do you have 20 minutes to speak with me sometime in the next week so that I can get your perspective?" (use this one only if you didn't already have an informational interview with her.)

Notice that in each of these examples, you're not asking directly for a referral or the opportunity to interview.

You're not asking the new connection to put her own reputation on the line for you before she is ready to do so.

Instead, you're asking her to help you *learn* more, to give you *advice* or *suggestions,* or to share her *perspective.* All of these will get you closer to your goal, because you'll be building one or more relationships within the firm—a critically important step to gaining the opportunity to work there.

If your new connection wants to go beyond your request and actually recommend you for the role, that's up to her. Make sure your request is appropriate and transparent and that you're willing to earn the next step. You may be surprised to find more doors opening for you! Especially if you follow the advice in the next chapter.

DON'T KNOW HOW TO SHOW YOUR GRATITUDE?

13

People want to be of service and you shouldn't feel shy about asking favors provided you keep the asks appropriate and remain willing to earn any real opportunities. But you won't be able to keep the relationship moving forward unless you close the loop on the favor. In other words, unless you say thank you.

Most people are aware of the importance of saying thank you. If you were subjected to Barney the Dinosaur as a child, you probably learned that "Thank you is a magic word because it's polite." Actually, it's two words, but who's counting?

It's true that saying thanks is polite. But it's far, far more than that. And most people don't really understand the phenomenal power of a properly delivered thank you.

Vivid appreciation, a process I will soon describe, is truly a magical skill. It turns a gift someone gave you into a gift you give back to them. When you thank someone in a way that they can fully appreciate and understand how their efforts benefited you and changed the world—no matter how trivially—you allow them to be inspired by themselves. This is a gift like no other in life.

SAYING A BETTER THANK YOU

Think about this in your own life. Did you ever give someone a really thoughtful gift? Or did you ever do something kind for someone—no matter how small or big? And then later, they came back and let you know how much it meant to them?

This is not the same as the thank you they said in the moment you gave the gift or did the deed. This is a later follow-up whereby they conveyed how your action impacted them over time.

You know what I'm talking about. Maybe you lent someone a book you thought they would like and they came back and told you how much it affected their life. Or you told someone about a great restaurant and they sent you a picture of the meal they really enjoyed there with a big thank you. Or you taught someone a few

PowerPoint tricks and they later told you how much time it saved them in making an important presentation deck. Take a moment to remember a specific instance of this in your own life.

Didn't that feel amazing? Didn't it further endear you to that friend? Didn't it make you want to go out and find another gift to give them or another deed to do, so you could continue that upward spiral of growing affinity and connection between you?

HUMANS HATE OPEN-ENDED CYCLES

Now consider a good deed without thanks. Did you ever do something nice for someone that they failed to follow up on with you? Maybe you recommended them for a job interview or introduced them to an esteemed colleague, and then you never found out what happened? That good deed went unacknowledged and the loop was never closed. In your experience, you may as well never have done the deed in the first place, and your friend missed an opportunity to deepen his or her relationship with you.

This is not about kudos or credit. If you were disappointed that your friend never followed up with you, it's probably not because you needed the ego boost of acknowledgement. Rather, it's because the circle of your own action didn't get closed, and you weren't able to enjoy the fruit of your efforts. You weren't able to share in the success, so from your perspective, your time went into a vacuum and never came out.

You can think of this as simple cause and effect. If you took an action, as a human being, you just can't help but want to know its effect. How did it turn out? How did the story end? Our reaction to this kind of open-ended chain of events and incomplete cause-and-effect loops can range from numbness to mild irritation to extreme frustration. But one thing is for sure—it's not a positive feeling.

This happens all the time in relationships. Frequently our actions and contributions go unacknowledged, and for the most part, it's not a big deal. We live with it.

But notice how much more willing you are to give to the people who recognize your contribution. Notice how much their acknowledgement endears you to them. Why not decide to be one of those people?

That means that whenever anyone contributes to you—whether they give you easy advice in passing or engage deeply over time—you MUST close the loop and acknowledge them. We call this particular kind of acknowledgement . . .

VIVID APPRECIATION

—

And I recommend you do it early and often.

Here's how it works. It has two parts:

1. Appreciation

Appreciation might be the very most important word in this entire book. Appreciation is the secret key to keeping good energy flowing to and through you. It's the key to unlocking the generosity of others.

You can never appreciate too much. I would even go so far as to recommend taking up Appreciation Journaling and cataloging every day in intimate detail all the aspects of your experience that you appreciated that day. You might be surprised at the effect this has on every facet of your life.

But with your friends, colleagues, and mentors, just privately appreciating them in your own mind or journal is not enough. You need to show your appreciation.

And you already know how to say thanks. It doesn't require a gift or a grand gesture. A few simple words can do it. Here are some words to try:

Thank you so much for _____.

I can't tell you how much I appreciate _____.

It meant to so much to me that you _____.

It made such a contribution to me when you _____.

You really made a difference in my life with your _____.

This first thank you part is pretty easy. The next part is a little trickier, but just as important.

2. Vivid Detail

Because talk is pretty cheap, even with one of the eloquent expressions above, if you stop there, your friend will not understand how they have benefited you. They won't necessarily be able to appreciate the effect of their actions, meaning that you aren't fully returning the gift to them and they aren't getting to share the success.

Consider these examples. Imagine you are on the receiving end of these communiques:

1. Thank you.

2. Thank you so much for your kind advice.

3. Thank you so much for your kind advice; it really meant a lot to me.

Each of these is better than the last—stronger and clearer in the mind of the listener, but consider this one:

1. Thank you so much for your kind advice; it really meant a lot to me because it was the thing I needed to hear to FINALLY understand what I was doing wrong in my communication with my team. The meeting I led after we spoke was night and day better than the last one, and I really appreciate that you were able to help me out with the perfect insight when I needed it.

Wouldn't you MUCH rather be on the receiving end of THIS kind of thank you? When you thank a friend in this way, you're completely closing the loop on their generosity, and you're giving it back to them.

For good measure, here are some more really simple examples of Vivid Appreciation:

1. Thank you for helping me with that problem set; now I really understand differential equations, and I got my first 100 on the last test!!

2. I just interviewed with Google!!! Without your introduction to Ralph, I don't think they would have even considered me. I can't thank you enough. I'll keep you posted!

3. If you hadn't shared your meeting notes, I wouldn't have caught the missing insight for my presentation. I really appreciate your help.

4. I can't thank you enough for your advice about fundraising for the club. We raised $2,000 at the event because of you!!!

5. Your feedback on my presentation style wasn't easy to hear at first, but I've worked hard to make real progress in my storytelling abilities, and my last client meeting was a huge success. Thank you so much for your generous guidance.

6. You told me about Andy's Thai Kitchen last month, and I have to tell you it has become my favorite Thai place. I've eaten there 5 times already. Can't thank you enough!!

It doesn't have to be wordy or complicated. The favor can be as small as a restaurant recommendation. But if you make the effort to show vivid appreciation, it's a gift back to the giver. It allows your professional friends to fully experience being of service, making a difference, and understanding their impact.

It turns a one-way favor into something shared by allowing the person who did the favor to be inspired by himself. Now we are deep into the third phase of the anatomy of a friendship: shared positive experiences.

13.1 Express Vivid Appreciation

Take a moment and think about your contacts. To whom would you like to show vivid appreciation? Consider your managers, supervisors, mentors, sponsors, champions, coworkers, peers, colleagues, friends, family, fellow club members, alumni, career services support staff, clients, even that guy at Starbucks who always remembers your drink order. List out all the people who have contributed to you.

Now take 20 minutes to send as many vivid appreciation messages as you can.

Add it to your calendar to follow up with the ones you'll see in person this week.

When you rise in the morning, give thanks for the light, for your life, for your strength. Give thanks for your food and for the joy of living. If you see no reason to give thanks, the fault lies in yourself.

—TECUMSEH

CONFUSED ABOUT HOW TO ADD VALUE TO YOUR NETWORK?

14

YOU KNOW YOU NEED TO
ADD VALUE. BUT HOW?

———

There's common wisdom out there in the transaction paradigm of networking that says you have to give before you take. I already talked about this in Chapter 1, so you know I think this is a load of hooey.

While the spirit behind this argument is true (i.e. generosity is a virtue), when it's framed this way—give first, then get—the true generosity is lost because it's all serving the end goal of getting. That's the very definition of selfishness and manipulation.

So the first problem you might have when you're trying to add value to the people in your network is that your agenda is getting in the way. This puts you back at square one. Go back and read Chapter 1 again, and remind yourself that deep, meaningful relationships are an end in themselves and not simply a means to get ahead.

Another problem you might have with this "give first, then take" concept is that you just don't know what you have to offer. The more senior and important your new contacts are, the harder it is to understand the value you can give them. A senior executive is a well-connected expert with very little spare time. Do you think forwarding that article you're obsessed with is really going to add to her life? Isn't it much more likely that it's going to be a time-wasting nuisance?

This is not to say that you should avoid sharing your information and knowledge with people senior to you! It's absolutely true that you have information that will be valuable to others—even senior folks. The point here is that one man's treasure is another man's trash: what adds value to one person's life is a waste of time for someone else.

And if you're still early in your career, you probably believe that almost all your treasure will be trash to those important senior people you encounter. And in one sense, you wouldn't be wrong about that.

GIVING SOMEONE THE CHANCE TO
BE OF SERVICE ALWAYS WORKS

———

The last two chapters have hopefully made it clear that one of the best things you can do for the people in your network is give them the chance to add value to your life and then follow up with vivid appreciation.

I am serious about this. Let people be of genuine service and then help them fully understand and experience the positive impact they have had. There's almost nothing better you can do for someone because this fulfills their very deepest desire to be meaningful in the world.

And it's probably a much more powerful value add to a senior professional than any article you might forward or introduction you might make.

But even if allowing someone to be of service to you is a great first step in bridging from a new connection to a genuine friendship, it can't be the ONLY step.

Because if a relationship doesn't have a future, it's not really a relationship. You'll need to find other ways to keep your relationships moving forward. Let's revisit the Anatomy of a Friendship.

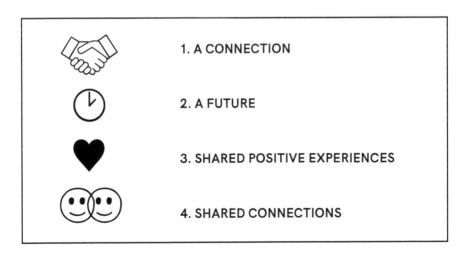

1. A CONNECTION

2. A FUTURE

3. SHARED POSITIVE EXPERIENCES

4. SHARED CONNECTIONS

Once you've mastered personal introductions, making new connections, giving them a future, and initiating those first few follow-ups, you move into phases 3 and 4 of a friendship: shared positive experiences and shared connections.

These two phases are more about sharing rather than exchanging, creating rather than dividing, and experiencing rather than reaching an outcome.

So consider that your job is not to add value or receive value, but rather to create shared positive experiences and shared connections. This, by the way, is the power of Vivid Appreciation. It takes the transaction out of a favor and turns it into a shared experience.

Shared experiences and shared connections are each an end in themselves. As you create more of them, you're naturally fostering a more understanding, empathetic, and interconnected world. Doesn't that sound like a worthwhile use of energy? Read on!

LET'S TALK ABOUT SHARED
POSITIVE EXPERIENCES FIRST

Shared positive experiences can take a million forms. Stop and think for a moment. Pick a close friend. What memories come to mind as you remember your friend?

If I do this exercise myself, I think of one of my lifelong best friends, fellow business school alumna, and travel buddy. She and I survived two years together at the University of Chicago's Graduate School of Business. We've visited over 12 countries together. We hiked the Inca Trail, drove through the desert, wilderness, and arctic tundra of Georgia (the country, not the state) and swam on beaches that could only be reached by boat in Turkey. Without a doubt, we've shared some of our life's greatest moments together.

Importantly, some of them involved struggle. The Inca Trail was a 4-day mountain climb. Neither of us are terribly athletic or fond of roughing it. The second night in the tent, interspersed with expletives, we solemnly swore that for our next trip we would go to a luxury resort instead.

During our first year of business school, we spent spring break in Rome. Having barely survived recruiting and an incredibly challenging curriculum, we were both exhausted. We ended up sleeping until 4PM every day, much to the chagrin of hotel management, who had to keep sending in embarrassed housekeepers to wake us up. We missed most of the sites in favor of slumber.

And throughout the years of our friendship, we've been there for each other through breakups, job transitions, family struggles, and health problems.

The thing that made these experiences positive, though, was that we shared them. We were both working together against nature to survive the Peruvian wilderness. We were both recuperating from MBA burnout in Rome. In life in general, when one of us was feeling low about our circumstances, the other one was there to sympathize and listen. In fact, if you think about your own friendships, some of the strongest bonds are formed by weathering hardship together.

So if you want to nurture and deepen true friendship, the thing that matters is that the experiences be shared. The more experiences you share and the more meaningful those experiences are, the stronger your friendships will be.

HOW TO START BUILDING SHARED POSITIVE EXPERIENCES

You're not going to trek Peru with someone you just met, and you're not going to spill your guts about family problems to someone you encountered last night at a networking event. You have to start small.

So far, all the things I've talked about in this book constitute shared positive experiences:

- Sharing an enthusiasm introduction

- Informing someone about something you love

- Listening to someone and asking questions that let them expand on a passion

- Conducting a great informational interview that gives them the chance to tell their own stories

- Giving someone the opportunity to be of service

- Expressing Vivid Appreciation

- Following up to let them know your progress

All of these things will create a shared positive experience because they create shared positive emotion. When you talk fervently about a passion, the listener is touched and uplifted, reminded of his own passions, and connected with his greater sense of purpose. You're both—in that moment—sharing a feeling of passion and possibility.

Something similar happens when you allow someone to be of service, thank them, and include them in your journey. The processes outlined in the previous chapters are designed to ensure your relationships begin with shared positive experience. And—very Importantly—these shared experiences can be created with anyone, anywhere, any time—no matter how different the other person may seem to be from you.

So, what are some ways to keep the shared positive experiences going? Well, here are a few simple examples of shared positive experience:

- Smiling

- Sharing a joke

- Finding a common interest

- Discovering a friend in common

- Learning something new from someone

- Teaching someone something you know

- Engaging in lively open-minded debate

- Connecting someone to someone else who can help them

- Sharing a favorite resource, book, class, etc.

- Growing together (for example, reading an article and discussing its implications)

- Supporting someone online (think retweeting, LinkedIn endorsements, positive Facebook comments)

- Sending an email on an important occasion

- Sending an email just to let them know you were thinking about them

- Introducing two people who don't know each other

The list goes on and on, but as you can see, these are all shared positive experiences that you could create with someone you just met. These small steps will naturally lead to the bigger ones. Not everyone will become a lifelong friend and travel buddy, but if you take time to create shared positive experiences with the people you meet, some of them will. And in the process, you'll be having a lot more fun with others.

THREE STRATEGIES FOR CREATING
SHARED POSITIVE EXPERIENCES

I know, you're busy. And often you're so focused on your own work and your own development that it's hard to take a step back and a deep breath and see how you can engage more meaningfully with the people around you.

So in addition to the tips above, let me help with three strategies for creating positive experiences with the people in your network:

1. Be kind

2. Be of service

3. Listen for shared opportunity

1.
BE KIND

Your first strategy for shared positive experience is being kind. It's really simple: just look for ways to be kind to others. To implement this strategy correctly, you need to treat everyone with respect and generosity, to give freely and without expecting anything in return.

I'm a big fan of the idea of random acts of kindness: just doing good deeds that can never be traced back to you. Some examples include leaving a great book on the subway, making an anonymous donation, or paying for the order of the person behind you at the drive thru. Anyone who has tried committing daily acts of random kindness will tell you it feels good.

But let's talk about Workplace Kindness.

Workplace Kindness is just adding an extra step of thoughtfulness and kindness to your daily work activities. Some simple examples:

1. Ask someone how they are and genuinely listen to their answer. Be there.

2. Say yes to someone who asks for help or a favor.

3. Teach someone something.

If you start to engage in daily acts of Workplace Kindness, you'll notice a few surprising things.

Life will start to seem easier. If you're focused on ways to be nice to others, it'll be harder to take your own frustrations too seriously and it will be easier to keep things in perspective.

People will start naturally returning the favors.

But most importantly, you'll get to know your contacts in a more personal way. To keep committing acts of kindness will require you to get to know them better.

Be kind whenever possible. It is always possible.

—DALAI LAMA

This is extremely important for developing true friendships in a professional environment. People promote the people they like. One of the best ways to be likeable is to turn professional colleagues into professional friends.

This doesn't mean you have to babysit their kids, play 18 holes of golf with them every weekend, or spend every Saturday night out on the town together. In fact, you never need to hang with them outside of work. But it does mean that you need to connect with them as complete human beings and not just as "boss," "subordinate," "peer," or "networking contact."

Here's an example of what I mean.

Think of a close friend. Could you name two or three things they like to eat? How about stuff they hate? If you were going to surprise your good friend with lunch, what would you get him?

This question is probably easy to answer for your close friends. You know their taste.

But what about the people in your office?

Let's try the Lunch Test

Take a moment and walk around your office. Take note of a few things:

- Which people do you feel you know really well?

- Who don't you know very well but wish you did?

- Who don't you know at all?

Then come back to your desk and try the Lunch Test:

- Ask yourself this question: if I were going to buy lunch for each of the people I saw on my walk, what would I get them?

- You might know who eats Paleo, who's avoiding gluten, and who's a vegetarian with a nut allergy. But if you wanted to really surprise them with something they love, could you do that?

In most cases, the answer is probably no. Food is always a great way to connect with people. Everybody's gotta eat, and most of us find great joy in a delicious meal.

To begin expanding your relationships with colleagues, use the Lunch Test. And then . . .

- Start to get curious about their tastes. What kind of food do they like? What's their favorite neighborhood restaurant?

- What's the one place around the corner they will never eat at again? What's their go-to splurge meal?

- What if you were going to take them out for ice cream? What flavor would they get? What flavors would they NEVER get?

But food is just one possible launching-off point. It's a good one, since it's on the outside of the safe Social Distance Circle. But deeper intimacy begins with curiosity. As you begin to get to know people better, you will learn what kind of movies they like, the hobbies that get them out on the weekend, and the aspect of their work that gets them out of bed every morning.

As you get to know your colleagues better as whole people, you'll naturally find that your relationships expand, your collaboration improves, and new opportunities will start to present themselves.

Want more ideas for Workplace Kindness to get you started being kind to the people in your network? Here are 34:

34 Acts of Workplace Kindness

1. Bring in breakfast for colleagues.

2. Email a compliment to a coworker.

3. Remember people's birthdays.

4. Let your boss know how much you appreciate him or her.

5. Leave a handwritten thank you note for someone who did you a favor.

6. Send flowers to the office manager.

7. Take 30 extra seconds to clean up the office bathroom sink before you leave.

8. Put sticky notes with positive slogans on the mirrors in restrooms.

9. Stop and listen.

10. Get coffee for your cube mate.

11. Congratulate someone on a positive life event.

12. Take a new hire out to lunch.

13. Email that person who's been waiting to hear from you.

14. Bring in fun office supplies for colleagues (think crazy color pens) to make the day more fun.

15. Get coffee for a busy manager.

16. Hold the elevator.

17. Say thank you to the office cleaning crew.

18. Thank a mentor and tell them how they've helped advance your career.

19. Relay kind words you heard about your friend to someone else.

20. Stop by and say hello.

21. Donate to a charity where your friend is a board member.

22. Keep an extra umbrella at work and let someone borrow it.

23. Cut a colleague some slack.

24. Surprise a peer with her favorite lunch delivered to her desk.

25. Say thank you to your boss's assistant.

26. Have a stack of postcards at your desk and write a friendly note to someone.

27. Ask someone what you can do to make their day easier and then do it.

28. Tell your boss about the great work of a colleague.

29. Give thoughtful constructive feedback to a subordinate.

30. Say yes to a small task no one else wants to do.

31. Say thank you to a busy executive assistant.

32. Say no to a request you can't fulfill, but thank the person for asking you and give a helpful suggestion for its completion through other means.

33. Reach out to a colleague you haven't talked to in a while (no matter how long it's been) and thank him or her for what s/he helped you learn.

34. Sing someone's praises when they aren't in the room (and when they are!)

Don't neglect online acts of kindness!!
Here are 12 more ideas:

LinkedIn

1. Endorse someone for an important skill.

2. Give a testimonial.

3. Say congrats when they get a promotion or achieve a work anniversary.

4. Send a happy birthday note.

5. Connect them to someone else in your network who works for a company they like.

Twitter

1. Retweet their important tweets.

2. Tweet articles they publish in your own feed.

3. Give them a shout out and let others know why they should follow too.

Facebook

1. Make thoughtful, positive, supportive comments on their posts.

2. Send a direct message on their birthday.

3. Post a "thinking of you" message to their wall.

4. Add their name to a comment in posts that you think would interest them.

As in any public forum, be sure to respect the boundaries of social distance. Don't risk sharing secrets or facts about someone that they don't want their network to know about. Be sure to use caution when making public gestures of support through online platforms. When in doubt, do not reveal any information about your friend. Instead, just react supportively to the information they share.

2.
BE OF SERVICE

———

Service happens at the intersection of what is needed and what you have to offer. Does the office filing system need a revamp? Does your club need a process for marketing to new members? Does your boss need help drafting a proposal? Does your team need someone to coordinate social events? Does the office head need someone to lead training on Excel macros? Do it.

Be of service to the people around you and the organizations you are a part of. It just feels good. The more you do this, the more you'll be creating shared positive experiences with people in your network.

To be of service, just look for places of need and then step in to fill them. As you do this, you'll begin to see places where you truly do have contributions to make, and—importantly—ones that align with your personal passions. When you serve others, you build trust and affinity, creating more opportunities for shared positive experience.

Need some ideas for ways to be of service to the people in your network? Here are 47:

47 Acts of Service

1. Email an insightful article with a quick synopsis.

2. Volunteer to collect silent auction items for an upcoming charity event.

3. Share your best practices with a peer.

4. Volunteer to teach a class on an area of expertise.

5. Give meaningful constructive feedback to someone when they ask for it.

6. Say yes to a small task no one else wants to do and do it well.

7. Bring in lunch to someone who's been working hard lately.

8. Share a list of your favorite technology tools with peers.

9. Introduce a newcomer to important members of your firm, school, or club.

10. Offer to pick up the slack on a challenging project.

11. Let someone know about an upcoming networking event you think they might like to attend.

12. Figure out the task you do best and offer to coach others in that skill.

13. Refer a friend for a job at your company and champion them through the process.

14. Set up a lunch-and-learn for peers to discuss success strategies within firm culture.

15. Do a quick internet search for solutions to a friend's problem.

16. Actively coach a struggling peer.

17. Show a new hire the best local lunch spots.

18. Compile a list of your 10 favorite local restaurants and share them with the team.

19. Ask someone what they need help with and then help.

20. Offer firm insider tips to a new hire.

21. Relay a compliment you heard about a colleague to a manager.

22. Get coffee for a colleague.

23. Donate to a subordinate's favorite charity.

24. Offer to pick up dinner for everyone who's working late.

25. Recommend a peer for promotion.

26. Take two colleagues out to lunch who don't know each other and introduce them.

27. Connect a friend to a valuable LinkedIn connection.

28. Offer to do the filing.

29. Step up to plan that benefit for your charity organization.

30. Visit the nearest soup kitchen and put in a few hours on the weekend; bring a colleague.

31. Find an organization that mentors youth on a skill you excel at.

32. Ask your boss what projects or tasks you can take off his plate.

33. Coordinate an office outing on the weekend.

34. Talk to people who work on different teams in your company and find out what they need help with.

35. Invite your friends to the benefit for the organization you serve.

36. Share your Excel macros.

37. Schedule lunch with a superior and a few colleagues to get to know each other better.

38. Make a PowerPoint guide to your city and share it with newcomers.

39. Find an organization that champions a cause you care about and contribute your business skills to a project.

40. Create a brief training deck on a new subject you're learning and share it with your colleagues.

41. Help a friend prepare for a job interview.

42. Defend someone behind closed doors when they're unjustly criticized.

43. Stay late to help a struggling peer or classmate.

44. Share your tips on success at the firms you have worked for with your network.

45. Think about how the way your team works could be more efficient and propose a streamlined process.

46. Attend a charity event when you are invited and bring friends.

47. Compile a list of top productivity hacks and share them with your network.

Service opportunities are endless. Find your favorites and be creative. The more you seek to serve your professional network, the more shared positive experiences you will create, and the deeper and more meaningful your professional friendships will become.

3.
CULTIVATING AN EAR FOR SHARED OPPORTUNITY

You start with kindness and move onto service. Both of these strategies focus on the present moment and on the people in front of you. They allow you to respond to people's needs in the moment, brighten their days, and contribute what they need. These strategies ask you to look around, think beyond yourself, and find concrete and spontaneous ways to improve the lives of everyone around you.

The final strategy to create shared positive experiences is to cultivate an ear for shared opportunity, or in other words, to approach every situation with this question in mind:

How could this be valuable to someone else?

When you look at life this way, you'll begin to see the hidden connections among people and things. As you go through life and work, you'll be more attuned to the ways in which the information or people you encounter could be useful not just to you, but also to others. You'll view things through the lens of possibility and interconnection, and as a result, create new shared positive experiences effortlessly and as a constant part of your life. Here's what I mean:

Let's say you just read an interesting article about developments in the field of neuroscience (notice this doesn't have to be about business. If you follow developments in specific fields because they're interesting to you, chances are they will be useful to someone else, too). Here are some questions you might ask yourself if you have an ear for shared opportunity:

- Would anyone I know appreciate the findings in this article?

- How do the ideas in this article relate specifically to the work being done by specific people I know?

- Whose opinion about or reaction to these ideas am I interested in hearing?

Or imagine you're meeting new people at a charity benefit. Here are some questions that might occur to you if you have an ear for shared opportunity:

Who should I tell about this organization?

- I just met someone in corporate finance in a consumer goods company. Who in my network wants to know more about that industry?

- The person next to me loves photography. Who else in my network is passionate about amateur photography and would enjoy talking to this person?

- The person I'm talking to needs a new mechanic. I don't have a car, but someone I know was bragging about their mechanic last week. Who was it?

If these are questions you would ask yourself, then making and sustaining new connections will come very naturally to you.

You would forward the neuroscience article to three friends in different industries and let them know why you think the information could be useful to them. You would ask the consumer goods financier if he would like to join you and your friend for coffee next

Wednesday afternoon. You would introduce your new contact to your colleague with the awesome mechanic.

Relationships naturally keep moving forward when you have an ear for shared opportunity, and it's this skill that'll begin to turn you into a social hub. You'll start to be the person in your network people turn to when they have a question or are looking for a resource. And this in turn means that people will be working to create new shared positive experiences with you, and the whole process will become an upward spiral.

Start thinking of yourself as a network instead of as an individual. Think: how can the people in my network benefit from what I'm learning/knowing? From this person I just met? From hearing about this opportunity I'm researching?

Contribute to others, and then watch what comes back to you from surprising sources. Be kind, be of service, seek shared opportunities and watch how quickly you cultivate meaningful professional friendships and—in the process—have much more fun at work.

14.1 Your added value

What are the top 5 ways you would like to add value to your network? What are the passions and interests you'd like to leverage to be of service to anyone you meet?

Go back to your enthusiasm lists. How can you turn your passions into value for others? Make a list of at least 3 pieces of content you could develop to share with your network and then go do it.

Here are some examples of what I mean

If you're passionate about your local restaurant scene . . .

Compile a list of your top 20 favorite restaurants with a description of the ambiance, the best dishes, and which kinds of events the venue is good for (large groups, client meetings, intimate gather) and include links to their website, TripAdvisor reviews, Google maps location. Publish this in a blog post, LinkedIn article, or even just a word document and have it ready to share with people you meet.

If you're passionate about global travel

Do a write-up of each trip you take—include hotel, sightseeing, and restaurant details. Have these ready to share with anyone interested in visiting those places.

If you love golf . . .

Review all the local golf courses and driving ranges you visit. Include insights about the best hours to avoid crowds and peak sun, and phone numbers for tee-time reservations.

If you like to cook . . .

Use Pinterest to track favorite recipes and invite new contacts to connect there.

Do a write up of your top five favorite _____ recipes and share it via email (fill in the blank with whatever you love—healthy breakfasts, vegan dinners, grill recipes, you name it—master a single narrow subject, try out different recipes and report the best to friends and colleagues).

Compile a list of your favorite cooking blogs or cookbooks with reviews and share them.

The possibilities are endless. And these are just hobby-based forms of expertise. The further you advance in your career, the more content you'll be able to create that shares your professional knowledge as well.

Starting with hobbies is easy, though, and since no one shares exactly your passions and experiences, there's a good bet that your Top 10 Restaurants or best local gyms list will be meaningful to everyone—including that CEO you're dying to create a next step with.

Start marshalling your passions to contribute to others. And then continue to develop yourself in areas of passion so you have even more to contribute. You're going to love this, and it's going to make your life more fun.

For more inspiration (and if you're ever planning a trip to Florence, Italy), check out my Florence PowerPoint for an example of sharing a passion. You can download it here: careerprotocol.com/florence.

WANT TO BECOME A SUPERCONNECTOR?

15

YOU MET, YOU CREATED A FUTURE, YOU CREATED SHARED EXPERIENCES, WHAT'S NEXT?

We're expanding on phases 3 and 4 of real friendship. In the last chapter we covered shared positive experiences in great depth, including over 100 ways to create shared positive experiences with members of your network.

You may have noticed that a lot of my suggestions included connecting members of your network to other members of your network. While sharing connections is certainly an act of both service and kindness, it's also an entirely separate component of a real friendship.

It's worth a moment to stop and consider the dictionary definition of the word "network."

Google: a group or system of *interconnected* people or things.

Merriam Webster: a group of people or organizations that are *closely connected* and that *work with each other.*

Dictionary.com: an *association* of individuals having a common interest, formed to provide *mutual* assistance, helpful information, or the like.

Notice the italicized words: interconnected, closely connected and working with each other, association providing mutual assistance.

Each of these definitions alludes to the defining feature of a network: that it requires the members to be *interconnected with each other.*

WHAT DOES THIS MEAN FOR YOUR NETWORK?

Well, it means that if you have eight friends who don't know each other, what you have are eight friends and not a network. For it to be a true network, at least some of your friends need to be connected to each other.

The beauty of networks is that they are not linear. If you have ever played Six Degrees of Kevin Bacon or even rummaged around in your LinkedIn network to find second- or third-degree connections, you know that the world is a deeply interconnected place.

But we don't always think about the power of mutual connections.

The way your brain works is a good metaphor for the power of a network. The human brain has about 100 billion individual neurons. That may seem like a lot, but consider that they are all interconnected. Each individual neuron can be linked to as many as 10,000 other neurons. That equates to more than 1,000 trillion relationships among the nodes of your brain, a number that is too large to contemplate.

It's the relationships among these neurons that determines how and how fast information is processed and reacted to; it's the interconnectedness of the neurons that gives the brain its power.

Or to put it graphically:

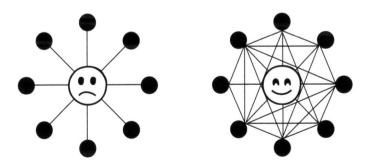

The right picture contains 35 1:1 relationships, far more than the eight represented in the one on the left. More relationships = more shared information, experiences, and possibility.

You can see that if we focus on filling up our contact databases or LinkedIn connections lists and view networking as just connecting one-on-one with other individuals, then we miss the whole point. The power of the network is amplified exponentially by interconnections.

This is also true of individual friendships, by the way.

Friendships grow deeper the more
connections they share.

DEEPEN RELATIONSHIPS BY
SHARING CONNECTIONS

If you think about it, you probably have the complaint a lot of people have about later-in-life friendships: they just aren't as deep and meaningful as the ones you formed during and before college. Undoubtedly the depth of friendships formed early in life is due in part to the fact that we have so many shared experiences with people earlier in life. It's also no doubt partly due to the fact that when we're younger, we're more open to others: we're still trying to figure out who we are, and the people who play a role in that process become eternally important to us.

That may be true, but there's another reason why friendships formed earlier in life have greater longevity. It's because they developed within a network. In our youth, we're still traveling in packs, forced by school and social activities into group environments on a daily basis. We are/were always spending time with multiple people and developing friendships with many people at once.

Let's say that on Friday you go to the movies with Ernesto, Ryan, and Amanda; Tuesday night, you study at the coffee shop with Ernesto, Ryan, and Carter; then, you lunch with Carter and Kevin on Wednesday followed by dinner with Kevin, Ryan, Amanda, and Jeni. Then, those people are all hanging out with each other without you too. In this environment, our awareness and appreciation for others evolves rapidly because we see them in a variety of contexts, with different personalities. We get to know them much better as a result of the variety of interactions. Trust develops more quickly and shared experiences multiply. This is part of what turns them into lifelong friends.

What most of us lose in our professional lives is this natural group context in which to build relationships. But that's OK, you can make this happen for yourself anyway. You do it by connecting the people in your network to each other.

If you're playing mini-golf this weekend with two work friends, invite a college friend and someone you met at a networking event to join. If you're checking out some live music Tuesday night, invite your friend's girlfriend, her friends, and a work colleague. Having coffee with an old friend who works near your office? Invite a work colleague to join.

I don't have to remind you to be sure to behave professionally in these situations, right? If you're worried non-professional shenanigans might ensue at the event in question, wait for another time to create shared connections.

SHARING CONNECTIONS ONLINE

Sharing connections through live interactions like coffee or mini-golf is still the best way to do it because—as humans—we love live human contact. But one of the great features of this global digital age is that we can reach and be connected to WAY more people than ever before, including the ones that we're primarily in touch with online.

LinkedIn and Facebook have created a very powerful way for us to create new shared connections. And email is a great way to introduce two people who don't know each other.

But since we're talking about cultivating genuine friendships, whatever way you choose to connect two people to each other, you must be thoughtful and invest in creating a shared positive experience for your two new friends, even if you're doing so via email or LinkedIn.

Let's take a closer look at what I mean.

THE AWESOME EMAIL INTRODUCTION

Imagine that you're connecting a subordinate, Laura, to a high-level manager, Jake, from your past job. Assume you've already asked Jake if it's OK to connect him with promising professionals when you come across them, or even with Laura specifically. But don't skip that step.

Always ask permission before facilitating a connection.

Consider these three options to make the introduction:

Option 1

Email to: Laura

Hey Laura, here is Jake's email address: jake@someemailplace.com. He's expecting your email. Follow up at whim!

Option 2

Email to: Laura and Jake

Hi Laura and Jake,

As promised, I am connecting you two. Enjoy!

Option 3

Email to: Laura and Jake

Hello my dear friends. I get to meet a lot of extraordinary people in my line of work, and it always gives me great pleasure when I have the chance to connect two of them to each other.

Jake is a former financier turned social entrepreneur via Awesome University's MBA. He's currently building a new social enterprise in India.

Laura is a recent Amazing College grad who grew up in Uganda, speaks five languages fluently, and has very big long-term social impact ambitions. She's already founded a successful nonprofit to aid education in her hometown.

You're both award-winning photographers, so I know you'll also personally enjoy speaking!

Jake, will you please tell Laura everything you know about finding work in the social impact space and what, if any, opportunities there might be for her with your company given that her own MBA is still at least three years away?

Thanks. Enjoy!

Clearly, you should choose Option 3. Here's what's great about it:

— This email actually deepens your individual relationship with each of them because it acknowledges what you appreciate about them.

— It creates an instant connection between them by virtue of their values and strengths. There's no doubt these two will follow up and become useful connections to each other.

— It makes it very easy for them to take the next step. They don't have to figure out what they're supposed to do—you've already created a future for them by suggesting the specific ways in which Jake can be useful to Laura.

How you introduce a new friend to a third person says a lot about how you value the relationship, and it's a very easy way for you to contribute to others—even those very senior to you.

I recommend you master the Awesome Email Introduction. If you do, you'll find ways to use it on a weekly or even daily basis. You'll strengthen the power of your network through interconnection, be of service to others, and take your professional friendships to a more meaningful level.

Get my email templates for awesome introductions here: careerprotocol.com/emails

If you combine this with an ear for shared opportunity, you'll soon be the person in your network everyone depends upon to inspire them and create new opportunities. That's a very cool person to be.

LOOK FOR OPPORTUNITIES
TO CONNECT PEOPLE

15.1 Who can you connect?

Take two minutes to think about two people in your network you can connect. Start with the people you see day in and day out. Choose one person. Ask yourself these two questions:

What is this person passionate about/ struggling with/ trying to learn/ attempting to achieve right now?

Who do I know that could help with that?

Then go out and make the introduction!

Ask each person's permission.

Send an awesome email introduction

Repeat as often as possible!

CLOSING WORDS

Oh my gosh, thank you for reading.

Now you have all the tools you need to go out and build real professional friendships in the most productive and graceful way possible. That means you can be confident in your charisma and connection abilities. And that means you can go out and create a more thriving networks of mutually supportive relationships. And *that* means you are helping fulfill one of my life missions: to make the world a more connected and compassionate place.

Ya see that? I tricked you into joining my team. :)

I hope you will take everything you learned here and use it to make your life more fun, your work more meaningful, and your network prouder to call you friend.

If you liked this book or anything in it, it would mean a lot to me if you'd take 38 seconds and leave me a review on Amazon. This way more people can help us fulfill that mission of connecting the world and making it a friendlier place for all of us.

Here's where you can do that: careerprotocol.com/verycool

THANK YOU!!!!

Angela

ABOUT THE AUTHOR

Angela Guido runs Career Protocol, the web's most refreshing destination for no-nonsense career advice and professional development services for emergent leaders and MBAs. Leveraging Angela's signature brutally honest but loving coaching style, she and her team have helped thousands of aspiring business leaders get into elite schools, achieve dream jobs, and have more impact and fun at work. Career Protocol clients and program graduates have gone to amazing places such as HBS, Chicago Booth, Google, BCG, McKinsey, and Goldman Sachs, among many others.

Angela has also created and taught programs for over 10,000 aspiring business leaders and MBAs all around the world, and her uplifting talks routinely get the highest overall speaker ratings at conferences and training events. Angela speaks to companies, schools, and associations throughout the world about storytelling, confidence, networking, and active career management. She's pretty funny too. And not just funny looking. Learn more about working with Angela and her team to achieve your professional goals at www.careerprotocol.com.

Printed in Great Britain
by Amazon

82319826R00086